GULLIBLE TRAVELS

GULLIBLE TRAVELS

The Truly Sensational, Humorous and Amazing Encounters of Over a Decade of Travels

Ronnie Bermann

Copyright © 2015 by Ronnie Bermann.

Library of Congress Control Number: 2015904142
ISBN: Hardcover   978-1-5035-5350-7
              Softcover   978-1-5035-5352-1
              eBook   978-1-5035-5351-4

All rights reserved. No part of this book may be reproduced or transmitted in any form or by any means, electronic or mechanical, including photocopying, recording, or by any information storage and retrieval system, without permission in writing from the copyright owner.

Any people depicted in stock imagery provided by Thinkstock are models, and such images are being used for illustrative purposes only.
Certain stock imagery © Thinkstock.

Print information available on the last page.

Rev. date: 03/16/2015

To order additional copies of this book, contact:
Xlibris
1-888-795-4274
www.Xlibris.com
Orders@Xlibris.com
684965

CONTENTS

Acknowledgments vii

Trip to Cancun, Mexico, May 8, 2007 to May 15, 2007 1
Trip to New York City 07-12-08 to 07-16-08 MLB All-Star
    Game, Yankee Stadium 7
Trip to Chicago 07-25–28-08 12
My Trip to Santo Domingo, Dominican Republic,
    December 27, 2010 to January 9, 2011 16
Trip to the Philippines Wednesday, March 30 to
    Wednesday, April 13, 2011 23
Chapter 13: Buffalo Encounters 33
Trip to Lake Powell and Monument Valley, Arizona to
    Utah September 6–September 14, 2011 37
Trip to Costa Rica Wednesday, November 23 to Sunday,
    November 27, 2011 49
Trip to Winter Park, Colorado NASTAR National
    Championships (By Invitation Only) March 22 to
    March 25, 2012 53
Ronnie Bermann's Baseball Tour June 11 to
    September 4, 2012 62
Trip to Myrtle Beach, South Carolina, April 12–17, 2013
    Monday After the Masters (MAM), April 15, 2013 142
MLB All-Star Trip Citi Field, NYC, 07-13-13 to 07-21-13 149
Trip to Bogotá and Cartagena, Colombia, 07-23-13 to
    07-29-13 The Good, the Bad, and the Ugly 158
Dove Hunting Trip Lake Brownwood, Texas 09-16 to
    09-18-13 166

Trip to New Orleans September 27 to October 1, 2013 169
Trip to Australia December 26, 2013 to January 17, 2014 176
Trip to San Pedro Island, Belize, and Roatán Island,
    Honduras, Central America May 28 to June 8, 2014 204

Acknowledgments

I would like to acknowledge the following people: Ludo Wurfbain, publisher in Safari Press, and Mrs. Berit Aagaard Pace, wife of Finn Aagaard, author of *Aagaard's Africa*, for allowing me to use the chapter in his book about my shooting a Cape buffalo.

A continuation from a previous journal that I didn't send because it wasn't interesting.

Trip to Cancun, Mexico, May 8, 2007 to May 15, 2007

First Day, 5-8-07

Met two girls at the airport who were going to Cancun also and coming back on the same day. I tried to call them twice but couldn't get them, so the next time I saw them was at the airport in Cancun. I have their names, and they live in San Anton, so I will try to get their numbers. I was picked up at the airport by Francisco (the son of Beatriz). We drove to his apartment. It was very simple and modest. He will be moving to Mexico City at the end of May to stay with his mother and help her part-time. When we got to his place, I changed, and we went out to go shopping. It was about 5:00 p.m. We drove to Playa del Carmen. Walked around on a street that was only for people. It was Fifth Street. There were only shops and restaurants. I bought two typical shirts and a cap. A friend of his, Elias, joined us. We ate dinner at about 9:00 p.m. We all had a lot to eat and drink by that time and were having a great time. The two guys were hilarious. We walked around some more until the clubs opened. We went to a club called the Blue Parrot, which was the best in Carmen. We had a great time. Got back to his place about 1:00 a.m. and crashed.

Second Day, Wednesday, 5-9-07

We are going diving with another friend, Ventura, at 2:00 p.m. in the town of Cozumel. We started out at 9:00 a.m., drove to Playa del Carmen, had a late breakfast then took a boat trip across to the island of Cozumel. Did some more shopping and met Ventura at his boat. The water was a beautiful green, turquoise, and deep blue and was very clear and warm. Ventura went over a few pointers and rules with me that were very helpful. Then we went into the water for my very first diving experience. He stayed with me at first, helping me and getting me adjusted. We saw many varieties of very colorful and different fish. The two guys tried to ride one stingray by grabbing the tail, but they missed. I just watched. Also, there was a turtle about the size of a night table, about two feet in diameter. There was also a five-pound lobster and a few very large fish. We stayed down for almost one hour, which Ventura said was about as long as possible with one tank of air. This was quite a compliment. The normal time to stay down for a beginner is thirty to forty-five minutes. We then got back on the boat and took our necessary one-hour rest after our first dive. We went back in for our second dive. I felt more comfortable this time. We saw a six- to eight-foot-long shark just lying still on the bottom. He finally swam away after a while. *Very cool*! We also saw another turtle about the same size as the shark. On this dive, I took my underwater camera with me and got some great pictures. We stayed down again for about the same amount of time. Each time we dove, it was in forty to fifty feet of water. It was about 6:00 p.m. at that time. We got back on the boat to take us back to Playa del Carmen. The boat trip took about thirty-five minutes. We both slept on the way back. We drove back to Cancun and had a late dinner at a very small restaurant in a hotel. It was very good. It also overlooked the bay. I almost forgot the most important thing. In Cozumel, before getting on the boat, we walked on the beach and saw some very nice young women without any tops on. It was probably not the last time to see that. We got back to the apartment and went to sleep.

Third Day, Thursday, 5-10-07

It was the official Mother's Day in Mexico. We planned a trip to the pyramids at Chichen Itza, about two hours by car. We get there about noon. The pyramids are all roped off so no one could climb them, but we walked around a lot and still saw a lot of the ruins and took a lot of pictures. We stopped to have a beer at a very nice hotel that was on the same land as the pyramids. The hotel was called Mayaland Resorts. After that, we went to three cenote caves with very large pools of clear cold water that you can swim in. They were very refreshing. At the first one, we could dive or jump from different heights. So I took the plunge from about ten feet above the water.

Francisco and I jumped together. It was a little scary. The second time was much better and easier. We drank a beer and a very refreshing drink out of a coconut. Then we headed back to Cancun. We changed and went to a nice small restaurant where he knew the owners. It was very good as usual. Got back to the apartment about midnight.

Fourth Day, Friday, 5-11-07

We went deep-sea fishing from 1:00 p.m. and got back at 7:00 p.m. from Cancun. There were five of us in total: one man from Houston, of all places; one couple from Scotland; and Francisco and me. The wife of the man from Scotland did not fish and was sick most of the time. There was supposed to be another couple, but they didn't make it on time. We were lucky they didn't show up.

We went about twenty miles out. The weather was beautiful as usual; the sea was slightly wavy. Francisco and I took a motion sickness pill before going. Beer and snacks were provided in the boat. We also brought a bottle of tequila along with us. We took turns fishing. Francisco and I were first. Almost immediately, we hooked on the same fish and reeled it in together. I don't think that happens often. Over all, we caught two mahi-mahi, three tunas, and one dorado. I had a big barracuda on the line and almost brought it in, but at the very end, it broke loose. The captain and his mate were very good. After each of our catches, we celebrated with a beer and a shot. The captain filleted all our fish and took them to the house of some people who Francisco knew and were having a party for their eighteen-year-old son on Sunday. It took us about one hour to get back to the dock, so we slept at the front of the boat. There was a beautiful sunset. After leaving the fish at the people's house, we went to eat at one of the best restaurants in Cancun, Puerto Madero, in the hotel district. It was very busy, and we saw some very interesting people. We got back about 1:00 a.m.

Fifth Day, Saturday, 5-12-07

We were going out so that I could complete my diving course. It was going to take two days. On my first day out (today), we went out with another couple who were already certified. The dive master and I just swam around for about forty minutes then came back to the beach and rested for one and half hours. We went back out and completed the first steps of my open water class. Successfully completing that phase, all that remained was Sunday to complete the course. It was 2:00 p.m., so Francisco and I drove to Puerto Morelos and had some beer. Then we drove to Akumal and had a small snack. Then we drove to Playa del Carmen and went to a cave that was turned into a restaurant, bar, and disco. Then we drove back to Cancun and had dinner at a restaurant we ate at before. Then we came home. It was another beautiful day.

Sixth Day, Sunday, 5-13-07

It was Mother's Day in the States. We went back to complete my diving course and get certified at last. We went to the same place that we went to on Saturday. We went out with two others, so we were four in total. We swam around for a while, and then the dive master and I went to the surface of the water where I was to perform my remaining maneuvers. Since I was not familiar with the technique of the maneuvers, I struggled a lot and got more and more frustrated and tired. We stayed in the water for another fifteen minutes, trying to stay afloat. I got back into the boat and got in. I found out that the dive master was seeing how I would handle stress. I guess because I didn't panic, I was OK. Then we went back to the beach for our rest time. We went back out again and swam around. This time, when we reached the surface, I was asked to do the same maneuvers as before, but this time, the dive master gave me much better instructions, and I had no problem completing them. ALL WAS WELL! We got back into the boat, and he congratulated me on passing the course and earning my certification. So I completed what I had set out to do while in Cancun. Then the fun started again. Francisco and I were invited to a friend's house for their son's eighteenth birthday. They were the people we brought the fish to that we caught the other day. As a gift, we brought them a bottle of tequila and three bottles of red wine, which we helped drink. There were about fifteen teenagers and about eight adults, including us. It was a very nice mix of people. One lady was from Cuba, and her husband was from Mexico. One lady was from Alabama, of all places. I think the others were from Mexico, but all of them spoke English.

So that was very nice for me. Even the kids spoke English. We got there about 3:00 p.m. and started eating and drinking right away. There was a lot to eat as appetizers, and at about 5:00 p.m., they started to grill some of the fish that we caught and some meat.

They let me help with the grilling, naturally. We took a lot of pictures during the entire time. It was a lot of fun. Since the next day was Monday, people started to leave, but Francisco and I stayed, so there were just the four of us until about 10:00 p.m. I had to suggest to him that it would be best for us to leave, so we did. We had a lot to drink, so we were feeling very good. We made it back to the house safely and went to bed. Francisco took most of the pictures and will send them to me. I hope they turn out good.

Seventh Day, Monday, 5-14-07

Maybe I'll do some shopping today, and I'm not sure what else. So far it has been one of the best, if not the best, trips. We went shopping in Cancun then went to Playa del Carmen to a topless beach called Merida Beach, one of the best nude beaches in the world. Of course we saw a lot of very nice young women. After taking a walk up and down the beach, we decided to settle in a certain spot. So we got two lounge chairs next to two ladies who were topless, but they were not too friendly, so we moved to another spot also next to two other topless ladies from Canada. I overheard them speaking French, so I started speaking to them in French. After about an hour and a few drinks with no result, we left and went to Playa del Carmen and walked around on Fifth Street again and went to some different bars and watched the people and had a few drinks. We stopped for dinner at about 11:00 p.m. Our luck had changed when we met two very nice and very friendly ladies. They invited us to their apartment for a few hours. What an unexpected pleasure. We both got lucky. Before leaving, we had one more drink at a bar and went back to Cancun. WHAT A DAY!

Eighth Day, Tuesday, 5-15-07

My last day in Cancun. Since my plane will be leaving at 5:00 p.m., we had a few hours to kill. So we did a little shopping, and there was a place where you can swim with dolphins. So of course I had to try that. It was fun and a new experience also. Francisco drove me to the airport and I left. WHAT A GREAT TRIP!

Trip to New York City
07-12-08 to 07-16-08
MLB All-Star Game, Yankee Stadium

Saturday, 7-12-08

Left Houston IAH at 8:00 p.m. Arrived in New York after midnight. Finally, I got a shuttle to Roosevelt Hotel where I was going to stay for one night. Arrived at about 3:00 a.m., Sunday—the thirteenth. Checked in to the hotel, left the hotel about 8:45 a.m., and went to Marriott Hotel East Side. Can only check in to the room at 10:30 a.m. Talked to two employees for about two hours until the room was ready. I got a lot of good information and how to get to the FanFest at Javits Center by bus.

Went to the FanFest and bought hats and pins, etc. The lines for other events were too long. I left there and walked to an outdoor café by the waters of Pier 84 on the Hudson River and sat down outside. It was a beautiful, sunny day. Had some white wine and a cigar. Went back to the hotel by bus.

Met with Larry and Barbara Mayer at 4:00 p.m. Was picked up at the hotel, drove downtown, and went to a BBQ-type restaurant that they knew about. We talked, ate, and drank for about a good four hours. Returned to the hotel at about 8:00 p.m. and picked up my tickets for the game in the hotel lobby. Went up to my room at about 9:00 p.m. and stayed there the rest of the night.

Monday, the fourteenth, was another very busy day. Went down to the lobby to make a reservation to return to the airport by shuttle and to get directions to Tavern on the Green to meet with Joannie Wecksler, a relative and traveling companion of mother's for a long time.

We met there at twelve noon for lunch. I took the subway for the first time ever. It was quite an experience. I met Joannie, and we started talking about family and so on with pictures that she brought. We talked for a long time before even ordering lunch. We finally ordered and continued talking.

At some time, a single lady was seated across from me, separated by a thin row of flowers. I didn't know who started the conversation with her. I think Joannie did. We continued talking and eating. I bought the lady a glass of Champagne. Her name was Courtney. She had never been to the Tavern, and she wanted to dine there before she left to go back to Oregon the very next day (just my luck). I did get her phone number, and I planned to call her soon. We had a very enjoyable three-hour lunch.

I also bought her lunch and a cap from the Tavern. I also bought myself a cap. We each wrote something on the other's cap. Then we all went our separate ways. I got back to the hotel in time to change and go back out again, this time with a friend that I've had for a long time but had not seen for a long while. We do call each other once a year because we have the same birthdays. Since I was coming to New York, I told her we should get together.

Aja Zanova was a world champion and a gold-medal figure skater. She was from the Czech Republic and defected to the USA when she was very young. She knew Dad from Maxim's when she was in town.

I went to her apartment in town. I brought her a red Stetson cowboy hat with hatband of small American flags that went all around the hat and a western belt with a special belt buckle from the HLSR. I think she really likes the hat a lot.

While we talked at her apartment, she opened a bottle of champagne. She showed me around the apartment with all the pictures of her with some very famous people and her many awards and medals. We were there for about one and a half hours.

We went to the very famous 21 club, where she is very well-known. We had a very great time eating and drinking and carrying on more conversations. At the end of our dinner, we were taken on a tour of the wine cellar, which was very impressive. We managed to close the place down. We walked back to her apartment and said good night.

Since I had heard of a bar named Don't Tell Mama, I had to go there. It was a bar where a lot of performers and other theater people hang out after their work. There was not much going on that night. I got back to my hotel room after midnight early Tuesday morning.

Tuesday, the Fifteenth

I went to the All-Star game. I left my room about 12:30 p.m. I took the subway to the Yankee Stadium. I got there about 1:00 p.m. I walked around the stadium to see what was going on. There was an area that was fenced off where people were standing around, waiting and hoping to see some of the players.

I was standing next to some guys and their kids that knew a lot about baseball and the players. They are the real fans. They all had their own personal tales about many of the players and their experiences and the games they had seen and so on. It was quite an experience listening to them. Of course, I had a few of my own, but not as good as theirs.

A kid just in front of me noticed one of the ESPN broadcasters and called him over to get his autograph. When he came over, I also got him to sign my Berkman Astros jersey that I had on. After that, I walked around a little because I was thirsty and had a beer. When I got back to the same place I was before, there was an NBC camera crew taping for the news that evening, so they came up to me and interviewed me and asked me some of the usual questions. They took some videos of me and my Astros jersey. I didn't know if I was on the local New York channel 4 station or not.

After that I went to stand in line to go into the stadium. When they opened the gate, I went straight to the area called Monument Park. That was where the large stones with the faces of four or five of the real great New York Yankee players like Babe Ruth and others are. It was quite impressive. Then I went to my seat. I snuck a pint-size plastic flask of Crown Royal into the stadium. I bought a large Sprite and added the Crown. It was very good, so I had another. The people around me had their kids with them, so they were very nice. BUT there were other fans who were a lot more vocal and visual and giving the other fans hell, booing the players and so on with their conversations and arm and hand signals with the other fans. Some of the fans were trying to encourage two very well-built ladies to dance and whatever else they could get them to do. Because the girls had a lot to drink, they were easily encouraged. It was quite funny hearing and seeing their exchanges. This too was a good part of the entertainment.

Oh yes, there was also a ball game. The two Astros players did very well. Lance Berkman drove in a run with a sacrifice fly ball. Almost everything started from the seventh inning on. The Boston Red Sox did most of the good things, but they were booed anyway. The ace reliever for the Yanks got the most cheers. The game lasted fifteen innings and was just under five hours. A Boston player hit a sacrifice fly ball to score the winning run, and he was still booed. I took the subway back to Grand Central Terminal, a few blocks from the hotel. I did find a small Japanese restaurant open, so I went in and had a late-night (early-morning) dinner.

I got to the hotel about 4:00 a.m., which was Wednesday, the sixteenth—the day I left. I got up at 8:00 a.m. and caught the shuttle to go to the airport. I got on the plane to Houston. I had a window seat this time, and the weather was clear this time. I was able to see the skyline of New York City and a lot more. WHAT A GREAT TRIP!

PS: I did ride the bus once and the subway for the first time. If it is your first time, and you don't have real, exact, and detailed directions, you can get very lost. It was a unique experience, and I'm sure if I had to, I would learn the system quickly. It is an amazing and ingenious web of tunnels that can transport millions of people a day. But of course, it can get unbearably crowded, like I experienced after the game.

Trip to Chicago
07-25–28-08

Friday, 07-25

Arrived in Chicago about 9:30 a.m. Got to the Hyatt Hotel and unpacked. A few minutes later, I got a call from Patti, the girl from Houston that I met at the Sail La Vie sailing club. She told me they were going to the boat. So I joined them. I stopped to buy a Cubs baseball cap. When I got there, there were about sixteen to eighteen people on the boat. After having a light lunch at the Chicago Yacht Club (CYC), we went back to the boat. We took the boat out and motored around for a while. Then we stopped a little ways past the other boats, and a bunch of us went for a swim in Lake Michigan, so I did also. It was great. The water was just slightly cold. Then we continued boating after that. We got in about 7:00 p.m. or so. I walked back to the Hyatt. That's when I found a wonderful bottle of Merlot and some cheese compliments from Dannille (she knew I liked that). What a touch of class. It came very handy later. I changed clothes and went to Morton's the Steakhouse, which was only a few blocks away. I really wasn't very hungry but felt like having a good steak. I also got a steak knife and fork and a napkin to add to my collection from Morton's (my third). Got back to the hotel and went to sleep.

Saturday, 07-26

About 10:00 a.m., I walked to a place called Navy Pier. It is a very long pier with very many attractions, including a huge Ferris wheel, restaurants, bars, things for kids to do, and also wares. There are a lot of the smaller cruise ships and other sightseeing watercrafts. I walked the entire length and back.

I called Patti to find out what the plans were going to be. At that time, her whole mood had changed, but I didn't know why. And I didn't ask. She didn't say anything, but I felt that something was wrong. I found out that the Cubs were playing, so I grabbed a cab and went to the game. It was almost noon at this time. What an incredible sight—the stadium, the atmosphere, the crowd, everything. The game lasted sixteen innings, but I left at the thirteenth.

Took the subway back to the CYC. It was about 5:00 p.m. by then. I walk to the CYC and got a wristband to be able to go on the dock. While I was walking on the dock, I passed a good number of other boats that weren't participating in the parade called the Venetian Night. By the way, this was the whole reason to go to Chicago in the first place. It is an annual event where about thirty or forty boats are made up to look like a certain theme, and the crew dresses up to match that theme. The boat where the person that I know was on was called *Whino Too*. They have won the competition each year for the past five or six years in a row, and they won it this year again.

The other boats were tied up at the docks and everyone was partying big time (I will get back to that later). Then when I got back to the *Whino Too*, Patti told me I was no longer welcome because I took a drink of wine from their own private bottle. At that time I had no idea how important this was to them and how bad it was of me to have done this. So I took a cab to a very good wine shop and bought them a bottle of their favorite wine and a bottle of some very fine French Champ. I got back in time to give it to them just before they shoved off. I apologized, but I have a feeling it wasn't good enough. I would not have been able to go out with them that night anyway. So I started walking back along the dock. This was where the fun really was!

I stood in front of a seventy-two-foot-long yacht called *Viking*. There were a lot of beautiful young people on board. I stood there for a while when one of the ladies asked me for my Cubs cap. So I gave it to her. Then I asked her if I could come aboard. She said yes and I did. Then the owner of the boat came over and asked me who I was. So I told him that the lady told me I could come aboard after giving her my cap. He looked at me for a few seconds and said, "You look harmless, you can stay."

There were a lot of beautiful young ladies and guys on board. After a short time, I became more relaxed, so I mixed myself a strong drink. The owner of the yacht, Jim, said he liked my turquoise nickels. I thought about it for a short time and then gave it to him. He was stunned and very pleasantly surprised. He even showed it to a lot of people. After that, I could do no wrong. He introduced me to a number of the ladies, but I was out of my league.

At about 9:00 or 10:00 p.m., there was a fireworks display. I had another drink or two. I don't know what time it was when I left the boat and walked back to the hotel. I was on the biggest, baddest boat there. What a day!

Sunday, 07-27

About twelve noon, I went back out. I first had to buy a new Cubs hat and a camera. I made my way back down to the dock to see if I could find the boat I was on last night. Sure enough, I did. Jim (the owner) and two friends were on the boat talking. I asked if I could join them. Of course they said yes. I sat with them for a while and had a beer. It sure tasted good. Then I went over to the

Whino Too to see if there was anything I could do to help clean up. They said no. So I went back to the *Viking* and stayed there. There were two young ladies from Prague that they had never met before, but I think they were friends of someone else who told them to go to the *Viking*. I'm just not sure. So there were six of us on the boat—four guys and the two girls.

We shoved off about 2:00 p.m. Now this is one of the best parts. As we headed out, we had to pass *Whino Too*. I waved to them as we went by. They saw me on board. With my other hand that was not in sight, I shot them the finger. We motored around the harbor until we found a spot called the Playpen where a lot of other boats were anchored. We spent the rest of the afternoon there. We also went for a swim in the lake. During that time, there were some other people from another boat that swam over to the *Viking*. They were very impressed. After a while, they swam back to their own boat. It was about 6:00 p.m. by then. We pulled up the anchor and headed back. They let the two ladies and me off at the dock we started out from. It was about 7:00 p.m. by then. I went back to the hotel and changed. I went to McCormick & Schmick's Seafood Restaurant for a good seafood dinner. It was good, and I was hungry because I hadn't eaten all day. Then I walked back to the hotel. It was about 11:00 p.m. by then.

Monday, 07-28

Checked out of the hotel at noon. I had time to have my pictures saved into two disks. That took about one hour, so I had time for some lunch. I found a very nice café and sat outside. I had a real good Chicago-style pizza. There was a very nice lady who was either the owner or manager that talked to me while I had lunch. She was quite attractive and personable. She gave me her card. If I go back to Chicago, I will go back to that restaurant and say hello—another unexpected pleasure. I picked up my disks, got on the shuttle bus, and went to the airport. The perfect ending to another incredible trip.

My Trip to Santo Domingo, Dominican Republic, December 27, 2010 to January 9, 2011

Left Houston on Monday. December 27, 2010. Arrived at Panama City, Panama, changed planes, and continued on to Santo Domingo. I was picked up at the airport by Mo. He was waiting there with a rum and coke for me. We drove to the Hotel Duque De Wellington where we were staying.

Moe had arrived on December 17. His job was finished for the year and started back on January 3, 2011. So he had to leave on the second. I was there until January 9. Moe had his girlfriend, who he had met on a previous trip, staying with him. We got together the next day, Tuesday, the twenty-eighth. We didn't do much at that time except walk around and saw some night life. On Wednesday, the twenty-ninth, a friend of Mo's by the name of Juan and his uncle, Harold, and I left Santo Domingo and went to Sosua (a small beach resort).

We started at 10:00 a.m. by bus and arrived in Sosua at 4:00 p.m. Juan wanted to be a musician and the uncle reminded me a little of the actor James Earl Jones with his mannerisms and his style of speaking. The uncle had reserved two separate hotel rooms, but when we got there, the hotel management misunderstood and only had one room available with two beds. So Juan took that room. The uncle and I found two other hotels close by. We got checked in and met a few minutes later and had something to eat at a restaurant that I liked a lot by the name of Morua Mai. (I don't know if it has any meaning.) I ate many meals there.

Later that same evening, the three of us got together again and did some nightclubbing. We also went to a place where Juan was supposed to play in one of the bands, but it didn't work out.

The Next Day, Thursday, December 30

Juan introduced me to a friend of his who would be my diving and fishing guide. His name was Raul. We set my first dive for Friday, December 31, at 9:00 a.m. He is a certified diver, so it was just the two of us diving. We went about forty to fifty feet down. The water was clear, but I've seen better.

While diving, I found an old bottle with a lot of sea stuff in it. So I brought it back with me. Later that day, Juan and I went walking on the beach where there were a lot of small shops and places to eat and drink. We went to a place of a friend of Juan's and had something to drink. I got back to my hotel about 6:00 p.m. Moe was supposed to arrive at about 1:00 p.m. for us to do a dive together at about 4:00 p.m. Finally, he and his girlfriend showed up after 6:00 p.m.

They checked into the same hotel that I was staying in. The three of us got together at 9:30 p.m. and took a taxi to another beach resort called Cabarete, about a ten-minute drive. This is where most of the action was for New Year's Eve. I was wearing a very shiny and colorful disco-type shirt, white pants, and a colorful knitted hat with the dreadlocks (long black ropelike hair) coming down out of it. Oh yes, and a pair of blue John Lennon–type sunglasses. Needless to say, I caused quite a stir. There were a lot of pictures taken with me, and I was asked to dance with a lot of people. What fun! We got back to our hotel about 2:30 a.m.

New Year's Day, Saturday, January 1, 2011

On NY day, Moe and I were supposed to go fishing. But when I knocked on his door, he said that he needed to take his girlfriend to the bus stop, so he didn't go with me. So I went by myself. I got to the meeting place at the beach, and since I already paid for Mo, I asked the young boy that I met the other day to go with me. There was another young couple from Canada, so there were four people all together.

The weather was very overcast, and it rained a few times while we were out, but at one time, not very much. The waves, on the other hand, were five to ten feet high. I almost got sick but didn't. We did catch five fish. I caught two. They all were good-sized fish. The fish we caught were called dorados, a very colorful fish in the water. I also had a marlin or sailfish on the line, but it got away. We were out from 8:00 a.m. till noon. When we got back to shore, we took a lot of pictures. I had one of the fish filleted and put it into the refrigerator in my hotel room. I went to the market and bought some things for me to eat and drink. Went back to the room, relaxed, watched some TV, ate and drank a little, and fell asleep. Moe and his girlfriend went back to Santo Domingo.

Sunday, January 2

Went fishing in the morning with Raul and his son. This time, we went bottom fishing for smaller fish. I didn't like that as much. The weather was much better, and we caught a few fish. I only went bottom fishing one other time.

Because I didn't start keeping a daily journal until later, I might be skipping around some things. There was one day I went to one of the small outdoor cafés of one of the people that I had met through Juan. My mission that day was to duplicate as close as possible the La Corona ad on TV with the guy and girl sitting in chairs with a bucket of Coronas with limes. Everything was easy to get. The only challenge was the girl. Directly in front of me were three married couples. Two of the ladies were good possibilities. So I approached the first couple since she was my number 1 pick.

Her husband could have played a defensive lineman for the NFL. Lucky for me, they all spoke English! I asked the husband in my most diplomatic way and at the same time explaining to them what I had in mind. He said to me, "You need to ask my wife." So I did, but she turned me down. Then I asked the second couple and she agreed.

By this time, there was a number of people gathering out of curiosity and taking pictures already, as well as the other three couples. I gave my camera to someone to take pictures of me, but they didn't come out. What a disappointment.

Back to fishing. I went out another day, but only in the afternoon from 1:00 p.m. to 5:00 p.m. There were four of us, but we only caught one fish. I guess fishing is better in the morning. I decided to go back to the hotel and call it a day. Since I had some leftover food from my favorite restaurant, I ate, had some wine, and watched TV.

The next day, I went back to Cabarete beach in the morning and spent the day there. As I was walking, there were two different couples that recognized me from fishing together and said hello. That was cool.

Oh yes, I had the fish filleted for me. My fishing guide, Raul, took me to his mother's small place on the beach in Sosua where she cooked the fish for me and served it with some beans, rice, and a salad. It was very tasty and all for about $1.50.

The weather after Saturday, the first, had been very good. Now today is Thursday. January 6. I went back out fishing at 8:00 a.m. There were three guys from Bermuda and one guy from Montreal,

Canada, that spoke French. He was very difficult. He even brought his own rods and reels. But he was told he couldn't use them.

We were out about one and a half hours when the motor overheated and stopped. So after a few tries to get it started again, they called for someone to pick us up and take us back. It was about 10:00 a.m. I went back to my hotel, changed, and went back to Cabarete beach where I began writing my journal. And as usual, I bought three caps and found three sticks that I will add to my collection. So I am caught up now. I had something to eat and drink while I was writing.

Later that afternoon, I went for a long walk along the beach. Then I took a motorbike taxi back to Sosua. I got back to my hotel in Sosua and relaxed a while before going out to eat at my favorite place. Then went to the casino. I went to the casino only twice. I lost about $30 each time.

Friday, January 7

I took the 8:30 bus back to Santo Domingo, which was another four-and-a-half-hour trip. I got back to the same hotel that I was in before. It was about 2:30 now. I got settled and relaxed for a while. Got up and went out to do some shopping. Went back to a familiar street that was for pedestrians only. I did sit down and have a glass of wine at one of the café bars that Moe and I had sat at before at the beginning of the trip. It's a very long street with many shops and café bars. Then I walked back to the hotel.

Saturday, January 9

After doing a few Aaron's at about 10:00 a.m., I decided to take a walk on the same pedestrian street. (This is where the day gets exciting!) I had noticed that the taxicabs had magnetic yellow signs on top of their cars. So as I was walking, I was always on the lookout for the possible ideal time to take one. Finally I spotted a strong possibility. The taxi was about ten to fifteen yards off on a side street while the taxi driver was sitting on the corner about fifteen yards away. I carefully tested the sign to see if it was magnetic, and it was. I waited for what I thought was a right time. So I went for it. I got the sign and started to walk away. I tucked the sign under my shirt. I got to a corner and turned and kept on walking. So far so good. I came to another corner and turned. I got back to the main pedestrian walkway and went up the street. So far so good. I went into a shop and got one of their shopping bags and put the sign into the bag and continued walking.

When I got to the end of the street, I sat down at one of the cafés that I had been to a few times and I ordered a glass of wine. After sitting there for some time, I became more relaxed. Shortly thereafter, a man that I had met several days ago saw me and sat down with me. He was quite a character, and he looked a lot like Richard Pryor. He was always trying to get girls to come over. I nicknamed him "Bird Dog" 'cause he was always on point. We sat and talked and drank for a few hours. Then I left and went back to the hotel.

There was some food I had left from the other night back in the room. The TV was finally fixed just in time to watch both NFL games.

Sunday, the Tenth

I flew back to Houston. But Sunday didn't go as smoothly as it should. My plane left at 6:30 a.m. The taxi picked me up at 4:15 a.m. There was an overturned truck on the freeway about six miles from the airport. That took about thirty minutes to get through. Got on the plane and it took off on time.

Shortly after takeoff, we heard over the loud speaker, "Is there anyone on board that is a doctor or has medical experience?" This meant that if that person had been very sick, we would have had to turn back. Luckily, the passenger was only airsick. So we continued on to Panama City.

Since my flight to Houston was on the Continental Airlines, I had to check in at the gate to be issued a new boarding pass (it gets more complicated now). She said that this flight was overbooked and if I would mind taking a later flight. I believe she told me that there was a seat on that flight. So I agreed to take the later flight. Since Moe was picking me up at the airport, I needed to let him know about the change. I did get him on the phone and told him of the change. But I overheard the lady say that the next flight was also overbooked, and I was on standby for that flight. So I got in line of the original flight, and when I got to the front of the line, she told me, "There IS a seat for you on this flight." I immediately called Moe to let him know I was arriving at the original time. And that was the end of my trip.

Trip to the Philippines
Wednesday, March 30 to
Wednesday, April 13, 2011

Left Houston at 9:10 p.m. My friend Mo drove me to the airport. Flew from Houston to Chicago. I thought that I left my cell phone behind when I went through security, but when I got back to Houston, I found it next to my phone in my apartment. On the flight to Chicago, I sat next to a very attractive but married lady. We talked practically the whole time. I think she liked me because of our conversation, and she gave me her card.

I arrived in Chicago about 11:45 p.m. Left Chicago at 1:00 a.m., Thursday, March 31. Landed in Seoul, South Korea, at 5:00 a.m., Friday, April 1. The flight took fifteen hours. The plane left Seoul at 8:45 a.m. and landed in Manila 11:25 a.m. Oh yes, Moe gave me four three-ounce plastic bottles that were filled with Vodka. I took them in my carry-on that was checked through security with no problem. We were testing them for future flights. One time, they asked me if I had any liquids, and I told them they were medicine, so they let me go. They did come in very handy.

The weather in Seoul was about seventy degrees and clear. Had about a four-hour layover (this time) before taking off for Manila. When I arrived in Manila and went through customs, I was met by one man that looked like a policeman. He approached me and asked if I was Mr. Bermann. I thought I was in trouble, but he escorted me to Sonia (my lady friend). I was very impressed. I took some pictures with him and another policeman. One of Sonia's sisters was there also. Sonia and I took a taxi, and the sister went on her way.

We checked in to the Manila Hotel, one of the oldest and finest hotels in Manila. We had a very nice view from our window. It overlooked the water, and we could see large ships docking and leaving.

The next day, Saturday, April 2, we flew to another small island and the city of Cebu and stayed for two days. We got here about 11:00 a.m. We found a resort hotel on the beach. It was nice but not great. I thought I could do a dive this afternoon, but I couldn't. When I talked to a man I would dive with, he told me it would cost me the same to do one dive as to do two dives. So I scheduled two dives with him on Sunday, the third, starting at 7:30 a.m. I will get back to that later.

Now I tried to do some fishing. I told the lady I was introduced to what I wanted and thought it was clear. She said to give her an hour to get everything together. When she got back, we got started. But the rods and bait she took on board didn't look right. I should have said something then, but I didn't. After a little while, I told them to go back in and refund my money. She didn't want to. I convinced her to give it back. So I talked to the guy about diving and signed up for two dives.

By now it was about 5:00 p.m., and since I didn't have much lunch, we decided to have dinner and a bottle of wine. After dinner, we took a walk on the beach. While walking, I found a bamboo stick to take back with me (as usual). It is now about 9:00 p.m. and time to go to bed.

It was now 5:30 a.m. on Sunday, April 3. I ordered a sandwich, some fruit, some water, and a six-pack of beer (to have after the second dive) to take with me. Before leaving the room, I turned on the TV. It was 6:00 a.m. here, and because of the time difference, I was able to watch the first half of the game between Butler and VCU. It was a very close game at the first half, but I didn't find out who won and the outcome of the other final four matches until I got back to Houston. I also missed the final round of the Masters Golf Tournament.

Back to the diving. We started out at 7:30 a.m. and got to the dive spot just after 8:00 a.m. The weather was great and the water was beautiful. No one else went with us; just me and the dive master and two men that stayed on the boat. Our first dive was near a small island. We dived down about thirty-five to forty feet, which was about the depth I liked. No need to go any farther! The water was almost warm and very clear. I saw a lot of very large fish near the surface and a lot of very colorful fish. I took a lot of pictures with my underwater camera. The dive master took some of me also. I was down for about forty minutes. When that dive was over, we moved to another location. The two boat crew and the dive master were all very helpful. One has to wait one and a half hours before diving again.

The second dive was not as interesting as the first dive but was also beautiful. We went down about the same depth as before. I stayed down for about fifty minutes this time. After the second dive, I could have a beer. I did some fishing for about one and a half hours but didn't catch anything except a slight sunburn.

Then I got back to the room and cleaned up. We took the sandwiches that I didn't eat on the boat and the beer back to the restaurant and had lunch. After lunch, we went to a shopping mall to buy a few things and look for a Filipino cap and found one. It's red and showing all the islands of the Philippines. Since I got back, I took it to a monogram shop to show the locations of the different islands I was at on the cap. When we got back to the resort, I had two margaritas and a very tasty shrimp appetizer. We went to bed. I didn't notice much night life here in Cebu.

It's now Monday, April 4. We woke up at 5:30 a.m. to catch our flight at 8:30 a.m. The airports were very unorganized, and it took much longer than it should to get checked in and go through security. We had to fly back to Manila and catch another flight to go to Legazpi, another city on another island. Looking out of the window of the plane, I could see a huge number of small islands.

When we got to Legazpi, we were met by one of her sisters and a niece. We were driven to another even smaller town, Oas, where Sonia had a house. We did make a stop to buy some groceries and some supplies. I also bought a pint of vodka and some cranberry juice along with two bottles of wine (and I'm glad I did). When we got to the home, there were a few other relatives living there also. The home is one step above the poverty level. They do have electricity—no air-conditioning except some electric fans that rotate. The toilet was flushed by pouring water into it. The water was collected in all kinds of containers when it is running only about two hours each night. The bed we slept in was a little wider than a single bed. To wash up, one had to use a washcloth and soap and then rinse yourself with water you would pour over yourself. I met some more of her relatives. We sat around and talked a bit and had something to drink. Then we had some dinner from the food I bought. After that, Sonia and I took a short walk around.

Tuesday, April 5

We roasted a whole pig. It started very early in the morning when a brother-in-law of Sonia's brought the live and not happy pig that was tied up to the house to show us. We then took it to where he lives to start the complete process. He also raises fighting cocks. There were two men that did almost all the work. They started by cutting its main artery under its neck and let it bleed to death.

It took some time for it to die. In the meantime, they put a large pot of water on a fire to come to a boil. When the pig was dead, they slowly poured the hot water over it, and the skin came off very easily. They did clean it very well. Then they took a knife and opened its belly and took out all its insides. They put in some lemongrass and sewed it up with some thin wire. Then they took about a twelve-foot-long pipe and rammed it up the pig's ass and out through its mouth. They secured both ends of the pig to the pipe so that when the pig was being rotated it wouldn't slip and would rotate also. The two men took turns rotating the pig. While they were doing that, a few of us went to the outdoor marketplace and bought fresh fish and a few more things to go with the feast. I also picked up about fourteen beers that some of us drank while the pig was roasting. It took a good three hours to roast it. The whole process took about five hours. When the pig was done, they laid it on a table and removed the pipe and began to cut it up. While the pig was still cooking, they put the six fish on a sheet of wire and cooked them. By this time, there were about twenty or more people that had gathered when they found out about the pig roast. I was a little disappointed with the taste and toughness of the pig, but it was a great experience anyway. There was more than enough food for everyone, and we had leftovers for another three days. They ate everything. After that, four of us went back to Legazpi to do some shopping again. We got back at around 5:30 p.m., and I made myself a drink then sat down for a few leftovers and some wine and went to bed. There is very little night life here either.

Wednesday, April 6

Today we did some sightseeing. We hired a van with a guide. He picked us up just after 8:00 a.m. Our first stop was the Mayon Volcano. It has erupted six or seven times over the last eight centuries. The most recent was in 1993 (not too long ago). One can see smoke or steam coming out from the top. We couldn't get too high up the mountain with the vehicle we were in, but we took some good pictures without any clouds covering the top. There were some hot springs that were covered up from the last eruption and some other points of interest that we couldn't go to anymore.

After that, we were taken to a waterfall. There were some fairly deep pools of water that looked very refreshing, but we didn't come prepared get wet; although I did walk behind the falls (that was fun). After that, we went to a very, very old church built in the 1400s. The volcano erupted on a Sunday, of all days, when everyone was at mass. The lava covered the whole town except for the bell tower. It killed over one thousand people. A part of the bell tower sticks up about thirty feet aboveground.

There was a young boy that would take pictures using your camera with a special technique. For instance, you would stand about eight to ten feet away and strike a pose like you were holding the stone. He would hold a stone up close to the camera where it looked like you were holding it. So I tried it on one of our people, and it worked. There were several other creative ideas that I can do, which I got from watching him. After that we went back to the small town where we were staying and did some grocery shopping and restocked on some more vodka, grapefruit juice, and wine. It's now about 5:30, and I sat down with a well-deserved drink! Then we ate and went to bed.

Thursday, April 7

Today was not nearly as active as yesterday. Today we took what they call a jeep, but it's not really a jeep. It's much longer and holds about twenty people sitting very close to each other. It was about the least expensive way to travel but not the fastest. It makes many stops and sometimes it stops for a long time. We went back to the town of Legazpi to try to change our flight to an early day. But it would have been too expensive, so we left it like it was. I did some shopping, and we had a bite to eat and headed back to her town. This time it took us two hours instead of one and a half hours. I had a beer and relaxed a bit. We went for a walk and came across the town tennis club. Sonia knew one of the tennis players and asked him if I could play tomorrow. He said yes and that he would lend me a racket and to show up about 5:00 p.m., Friday. I was looking forward to this. I hadn't played tennis in a very long time. So this was going to be fun.

Friday, April 8

We got up at 7:30 a.m. and had some breakfast and went to the open marketplace and bought some tilapia fish and other food. We went to another town with a larger market and a larger selection. I bought another bottle of wine and some other things we couldn't get at the smaller market. By the time we got back, it was time for lunch. We had a good lunch with the things we bought.

It was arranged for us to see a cock fight. There were a lot of people with their fighting cocks and a lot of bystanders. There were some of the people with their cocks, holding them up against the other cocks to get them in the fighting mood. You pay to enter and see one fight—two people with their cocks facing each other ready to fight. Before the fight began, there were about eight or ten men that came into the ring. The ring was about twenty-five feet in diameter with bars like a cage going up about twenty feet. The men are taking bets by holding up different number of fingers on each hand. I have no idea what it means, but I'm sure they do.

The fight didn't last very long. The winning cock had the pleasure of finishing off the losing cock. Oh yes, there was a sign that was painted on the wall where they hold the fight that reads Animal Health Care.

We were driven back to Sonia's house. I took a two-hour rest. Then we went back to the tennis club for my second tennis practice session. Sonia took a lot of pictures. It was a lot of fun, and the people had some good laughs. When we got back to her house, I cleaned up and sat down and had a beer and relaxed awhile before eating. Now I'm sitting on the porch with a glass of wine and writing in my journal as I did almost always at the end of the day.

Saturday, April 9

The usual—got up at 7:30 a.m., had breakfast, sat around, and talked for a while. We found out there is a basketball tournament being held today, so we went to the covered basketball civic center. The teams were composed of the best high school players from that particular district or town. Like an all-star team. I must say some of them were very good. We watched two games. After the last game, I saw the winning team that I was rooting for gathering on the street, so I went over to them and had my picture taken with them with all our hands joined together in the middle, like I was part of the team. The coach asked if I would send him a copy. So I made an eight-by-ten picture of it and sent it to him. We went back to the house for lunch. Saturday was the only day it rained, but just slightly, most of the day. Later that afternoon, we did some shopping and visited the grave of Sonia's parents.

They did have a small TV, so I watched some of the Masters Golf Tournament. It was Saturday here but Friday in the States. There is a ten-hour difference in time. At this time, it was the second round, and Tiger was three strokes off the lead. When I got back to Houston, I was able to see highlights of the game.

We ate dinner at 7:00 p.m. At eight, we went to watch a talent show at the civic center. The contestants ranged from ages six years to their thirties. Luckily, it started to rain harder so we left.

Sunday, April 10

We flew back to Manila. We checked in to a hotel named Maxims, a brand-new and very upscale five-star hotel with casinos on three floors, a very exclusive shopping mall, a theater, and some food courts and other restaurants. All the rooms were suites. The least expensive one was $300 per night. So I gladly took that one after the living conditions I was in for a week.

It was 5:00 p.m. when we arrived, and after we got settled, we took a taxi to a high-rise apartment where Sonia owned a unit. It was a small unfurnished two-bedroom unit. She does not stay there, so she didn't have the electricity or the water turned on yet. We got back to the hotel and ate dinner. After that, we walked around the casino, and of course, after a while I sat down—first at a slot machine and won about 50¢. Then I sat down at a blackjack table and won about $35. I lost it all back and more the next day. We walked to the lounge area where they had entertainment, so we hung out there for a few hours. They had a lot of very good entertainers. We went to bed at about 1:00 a.m.

Monday Morning, the Eleventh

Got up at about 10:00 a.m. and had our complimentary breakfast. We walked around the mall for a long while just to kill some time. We also went back to the lounge and listened to a young Asian girl singer who was accompanied by an older black guitar player and singer. Finally it was time to leave the hotel and meet friends and relatives that came into town to say hello. So we met at a small restaurant for dinner. There were about twenty of them, and they stuck me with the check. Then we went to the airport, and they dropped me off.

When I got to the airport, it was too early to check in for my flight, so I had to wait. I was one of the first in line, and it was a good thing because when I showed my ticket to the lady (this is where it gets complicated), she told me that my flight was for 12:10 a.m. on the eleventh, and now it was going to be 12:10 a.m. on the twelfth. So I was twenty-four hours late for my flight. Luckily, she was able to book me on the same exact flight with all the same schedules without any fees. So I got back to Houston twenty-four hours later. I did have an eleven-hour layover in Seoul, South Korea.

I arrived in Seoul very early in the morning. I found some comfortable chairs and slept for a few hours. There is a very nice lounge next to where I was called the Hub Lounge. They charged $23 to enter for all-you-can-eat and drink. There was a buffet and also wine, vodka, Johnny Walker scotch, white and red wine, and beer on tap. Also some comfortable sofas and a TV screen. I got my money's worth. I stayed there for about five hours. I left there and went to my gate to board my plain to Los Angeles. The flight took eleven hours. We arrived in Los Angeles at 9:00 a.m. We went through the customs there. I had two bamboo sticks with me that they wouldn't allow me to take in. We took off at 5:00 p.m. The flight wasn't full, so I sat next to the window and enjoyed the scenery as long as it was still light. I was able to get in touch with Moe to let him know about my new arrival. He met me and took me home. Overall, it was a good trip—had a lot of fun, met a lot of nice people, saw a lot of interesting sites, etc.—but would not do it again.

Chapter 13

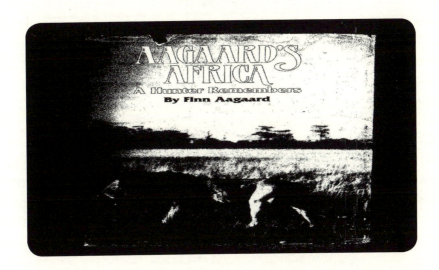

Buffalo Encounters

Taken from the book Aagaard's Africa:
A Hunter Remembers by Finn Aagaard

If you were to ask him, Ronnie Berman, who runs one of Houston's best restaurants, would probably tell you that there is nothing much to hunting buffalo – a chap simply goes a little way out of camp and shoots one.

When Ronnie came on safari with us in 1976, he had never fired a shot at any sort of four-footed game whatsoever. But Leonard

Burke, his mentor and companion on the hunt, had taken him out to the range many times, and had so drilled and practiced him that Ronnie handled a rifle safely and very competently. He shot quite well, too, even with the .375 H & H Magnum that Len lent him.

We made our first camp in the cool forests of the rolling Loita Hills, at the edge of the trees overlooking a long open valley near Entasekera, at about 7,000 feet elevation. We arrived in mid-afternoon, and by 5:00 p.m. were all settled in, camp pitched, the rifles sighted in and afternoon tea quaffed. I suggested that we might drive around a little to get the feel of the country and perhaps find tracks or other indications that would give us some hint as to where we should start hunting on the morrow. Almost as an afterthought, I suggested that we might as well take our rifles along with us.

Kinuno stood in the back of the Land Rover station wagon with his head out of the roof hatch, but the rest of us were not paying much attention. Len and I were reminiscing, for Ronnie's benefit, about our first hunt together, some five years previously. Then, Len had been the neophyte and a smallish zebra that we bagged the opening morning of the hunt was the very first game animal larger than a rabbit that he had ever taken. But, by the end of a wonderful three-week safari he was a veteran, with two buffalos and an elephant to his credit, and both he and his vivacious wife, Connie, had fallen so much in love with Africa that they had come back to some part of it every year since.

"*Sumama, Bwana – Nyati!*" Kinuno urgently and accusingly broke in on our yakking, commanding me to stop because he had seen a buffalo. Sure enough, a patch of forest grew along the crest of the otherwise open ridge across the valley from our position and a huge, grizzled, old buffalo bull had emerged from the trees to graze in the open during the cool of the evening. The massiveness of its horns was quite apparent even to the naked eye and I did not have to study it for long before reaching a decision.

"Darn it," I said to Ronnie. "I had planned to break you in gently on an impala or something equally innocuous, but that fellow is much too good for us to pass up. Bring the .375 and follow me."

Luckily, our side of the valley was timbered, so we just went straight down it under cover and started up the other side. Though it was open grassland, the opposite slope was so convex that we could see no more than about 30 yards ahead. Nearing the top, we went very slowly until I caught a flicker of movement up ahead. It was the bull, swishing his tail at an insect. I grabbed Ronnie's arm and motioned for him to imitate my crouch as we duck-walked forward another 20 feet. Then we stood up quickly, while with practiced swiftness Kinuno planted the crossed shooting sticks in front of Ronnie and indicated that he should lay the rifle in the crotch. The surprised bull raised his head to stare, standing with his body turned almost but not quite straight towards us, and startled into a fleeting immobility. I touched Ronnie on the collar bone, between neck and shoulder.

"Hit it right there," I commanded in a whisper. "Shoot now!"

I hardly heard the roar of the .375, but was astounded to see the bull simply collapse and roll over with all four feet in the air when the 300-gr. Winchester "solid" bullet thumped home. It was so unexpected – buffalos never drop in their tracks – that I must have stood there gaping for almost a whole second before remembering to tell Ronnie to shoot it again, as is customary and wise. It was redundant in this case, but old professionals don't attain that status by taking unnecessary chances.

The whole episode was utterly incredible. This kid, on his first afternoon out of Nairobi, rides for 20 minutes in the Land Rover, walks perhaps half a mile and clobbers a monstrous old buffalo, which just rolls over in its tracks, as dead as the proverbial kippered herring. Not only is it the first game of any sort he has ever taken, but it is also a tremendous trophy, with massive bosses and deep curls that sweep around to give a 4 ½ - inch spread. Many a man has spent weary weeks of travail on several different safaris looking for a decent buffalo without getting anything nearly as good.

Later in the hunt we spent most of two days trying to get a shot at one particularly handsome, and very elusive, impala buck. So Ronnie might tell you that buffalos are a piece of cake, but that impalas are a real challenge. Not everyone would agree with him, of course, in fact hardly anyone would. Len certainly knew better, as we had a trifling amount of excitement with the two buffalos taken on his original hunt.

Trip to Lake Powell and Monument Valley, Arizona to Utah September 6–September 14, 2011

September 6

Ron took me to the airport. The plane left at 8:40 a.m. and landed on Phoenix, Arizona, at 9:30 a.m. My next connection was at 12:45. I needed to claim my luggage and have it transferred to my next flight to Page, Arizona. I had plenty of time to do that. I went ahead and took care of that and still had time for a glass or two of wine and Arizona's finest fried shrimp basket.

Phoenix is two hours earlier than Houston. The plane from Phoenix to Page, Arizona, was a two-propeller plane. Since all the passengers and crew were there, we took off about twenty-five minutes early. What a unique idea. There was a crusty old lady with a gruff voice that I struck up a conversation with. When we got on the plane, she was sitting in a seat with no one in the seat in front of her. So she pushed that seat back down where it was possible for her to prop her feet up. This was totally new to me. So I did the same.

The flight lasted one hour. I contacted the car rental agency to let them know that I have arrived like I was instructed and because it only took about five minutes for him to get here. The car was a four-wheel-drive Jeep. I had requested that because I intended to do some off-the-road driving. He went over a lot of important details with me before cutting me loose. This was all very important. So about 2:00 p.m., I left his place. My first stop, as usual, was to stock up on things to eat and drink and a cooler to keep them in when necessary. I used the cooler often. The temperature in Page at the time was a very comfortable eighty degrees and dry.

After shopping, I drove to the Lake Powell Resort, only about ten minutes away. One of my goals was to get caps and sticks (to make into walking sticks) from the different areas I've been in. I was able to get two caps of the areas while I was shopping. After getting settled, I went walking toward the lake. There was a lot of tall brush off to the side, so I headed over there in hopes of finding a suitable walking stick to add to my collection. Number 1 stick found. While walking, I spotted three wild rabbits. It was getting dark about now. I saw a P2 fire that was coming from the pool area. There was a real nice outdoor fire pit. I went back to my room and brought back something to eat and some wine. My supplies were already paying off. While I was enjoying my snack and wine, I started my journal. I didn't complete it that night because it was getting late.

Wednesday, September 7

After finishing the first day's journal, I gathered everything I needed to go on my first of four boat cruises. Gathering everything I needed meant a container of margaritas, a few beers, some wine—just in case—and a sandwich. We started lining up at 8:30 a.m. and walked down the hill to the marina to board the boat for the cruise. We left at 9:00 a.m. We could sit outside on the top deck or inside below deck. When we boarded the boat, we were given headsets that told us all the important things on the tour in four different languages. I chose to sit outside.

There was a man from Hershey, Pennsylvania, sitting next to me. His name was Chuck. His wife was sitting just across the aisle from us. After we got under way, I asked him if he wanted something to drink. He said yes. So we had some margaritas (they were a bit strong). After a few sips, he became very talkative. He was a retired math professor at a university in Pennsylvania. He also knew a lot about Indian lore and history. Between telling us the history of the lake on our headsets, there was Indian music and chanting. So my new friend started singing and chanting along but NOT in a loud way. I joined in with him. He told me his Indian name was Smiling Fox because he was always smiling and was as smart as a fox. He gave me the name of Funny Water. You figure it out. Needless to say, we had a good time. There was a lady in front of us that was a bit upset. The other passengers didn't have any problem with it.

I took a lot of pictures. The cruise took about three hours. I got back to my room and started to call around to book a fishing trip with a fishing guide. I finally found what I wanted. So I booked two days with him. My second boat cruise of the day was at 4:15 p.m. until 5:45 p.m. Once more, I was well prepared with my cooler. There was a lady that I shared a beer with and that was fine. The absolute best part was on the cruise when I noticed a young French girl with a very poor imitation of a cowboy hat made of straw. I told her in French that I could shape it much better to look more like a cowboy hat. And she had a young friend with the same hat. So they agreed to let me reshape their hats. After I reshaped them and the reshaping was very successful, the hats looked a lot better. We continued talking in French at times. We talked for the entire cruise. I think the rest of the passengers were very caught up in our conversation. I taught them a few expressions and slangs of Texans. I did have my picture taken with them. These are times I wish Ron was here. After the cruise was over, I went to my room and changed into my bathing suit and went for a quick swim. As usual, I brought my cooler with me with the usual. So far the weather has been perfect.

Thursday, September 8

On Thursday morning, I had nothing planned. It was an open day. I drove back into town for some supplies and a fishing license that I needed for my next two days of fishing. And because the guide only takes cash, I went to an ATM machine. I was able to take care of all this at the Walmart. On the way back, there was a bridge and a dam. There was a visitor's center there. So I went in and bought a ticket for the tour of the dam. It was very interesting, and it told everything about the dam. I took a lot of pictures. The tour lasted forty-five minutes. I drove back toward the resort but went past it because the place I am to meet the fishing guide is at a place called Stateline Boat Launch. It is actually in Utah.

On the way to Stateline, I saw a sign for a beach and swimming. So I turned there and parked. There was a short walk to the beach area. It was only about noon then, so I went back to my room and fell asleep for two hours. I got up and put on my bathing suit and brought my trusty cooler that has become very handy. When I got back to the beach, I took a quick swim. The water was only a little cool on the surface and much colder at deeper depths (here it gets interesting again).

I was relaxing on my towel when a lady comes walking by. She works at the resort and was off for the day. We said hello. I asked her if she would like to join me, so she sat down. She was in her midforties. She told me all about herself. I offered her some wine and she accepted. She liked the wine and drank a good amount. She is very artistic and knows a lot about rock formations, etc. She lives in Tucson, Arizona, where she had a shop where she sold the rocks and things she has found. It was getting dark about now, so I took her back to where she lived (much more about her later). Of course I told her a bit about myself and that I was staying at the resort and my room number. I went back to my room for the night. I watched some of the Thursday Night Football game between Green Bay Packers and the New Orleans Saints.

Friday, September 9

The day started very early because the third of my boat cruises started at 7:30 a.m. It was the longest of the boat tours and the most beautiful. Our destination was Rainbow Bridge. The day started a little cooler and a bit overcast. But the sun came out, so it warmed up around noon. The canyon and rivers were discovered in the 1700s. A huge amount of history. The actual lake came into existence in 1957 when the dam was started and only completed in 1963 and took over fifteen years to fill up. Rainbow Bridge is a giant archway made out of one gigantic piece of stone. We had to walk about one-fourth mile. One could see the bridge from a distance, and it looks bigger as you get closer. On the walk to the bridge, I came across a long thin snake. It startled me. I was able to show it to someone, and they identified it as a garter snake (nonpoisonous). We had about one hour to look around. There was a park ranger that talked to us and gave us some history along with some pictures of some very famous people that have been here from a long time ago. Before the tour began, we were given some strict rules to follow. While the ranger was talking to the group and walking around, I got to know another man who was somewhat like me. If you tell us we can't do something, that is the first thing we will do. I found out that he was in the Army Air Corps Parachute Division and served in Vietnam. So when we got back to the boat, I asked him if he would like to have a beer. So we had a few. Since it was a bit hotter on the way back, there were fewer people on the top deck. We got back about 1:00 p.m. I went to my room and had some lunch and went to sleep for a few hours. At 4:30 p.m., I went down to take my last boat tour. We started at 5:00 p.m. They served a three-course dinner—salad, main course, and dessert. I chose the trout for my main course. I brought a container of white wine with me and concealed it.

There was a very nice couple sitting with me from DC. We got back in at 7:00 p.m. I did forget to mention that there have been a good number of very well-known motion pictures filmed on Lake Powell such as *The Ten Commandments, The Robe, Planet of the Apes, Broken Arrow,* just to name a few.

Saturday, September 10

I am writing today what happened the day before because yesterday was a very long and tiring day. It was about 8:00 a.m. and I finished the previous day's journal. Today I plan to drive to Monument Valley. It is about a two-and-a-half-hour trip. I got directions from the front deck. The first part of the directions (getting out of town) was, to me, the hard part. So I stopped to get directions. After that it was easy.

After driving quite a long way, I started glancing off the side of the road to possibly spot a good stick I could bring back. I made several stops and finally found one that I thought was suitable but was not up to my expectations. I kept it just in case because I didn't know what I would find in Monument Valley.

As I got closer to Monument Valley, I started to see some incredible rock or mountain formations. This is where my off-the-road Jeep's four-wheel drive came in handy. When I saw a break or entrance in the fence line, I took it and was able to get a lot closer to the huge formation and I was always on the lookout for a stick. I limited my off-the-road driving to where there were some tire tracks. When I got the picture that I wanted, I turned back. I did go off the road a few times more before getting to MV. I did find two more sticks that were a little better then the first one but still not quite good enough.

I finally got to MV. I had crossed over in to Utah now. At the end of the highway, it branched off to the left and took you to a well-known resort by the name of Goulding's Lodge. That was only one mile. I found a place to park. I got out and walked around a bit to see what there was to see. There was an awesome sight, three mountains, behind me, so I had someone take a picture of me and the mountains. I walked a little and saw an old stagecoach, so I climbed up on it and had someone take a picture of me with the mountains in the background.

There was also a small room that had a few pictures of John Wayne and other stars from some films that he was in. I think that helped to make MV famous. After that I walked back to my Jeep since I had my cooler with me with the usual. I ate lunch and had a beer. I left there and drove to MV—about five miles away. As I entered MV Park, I got a map of the area. When I saw the route I wanted to take, I headed out. I did stay on the designated route until I saw another off-the-road trail and took it. Again, this enabled me to get closer to the incredible mountain, AND I did actually find the perfect stick from MV. I will treat this one differently from the others. I planned to put it into a shadow box with a pack on it and hang it up.

Getting back to the original road was a little difficult now because I got turned around a bit. I continued upward. I came to an area that had a stable with some horses and three or four colts. I had my picture taken with them. One could only go about ten miles per hour because of the bad condition of the road. I finally made it back to the highway and headed back to Page, Arizona. Since I had found the perfect stick, I threw the others away. When I got back to Page, I stopped at the Walmart and bought a Top Ramen (instant soup).

It was almost dark when I got back to the resort. I found a way to get the soup good and hot. When I got settled, I had the soup and some well-needed wine. I was able to catch the fourth quarter of the Michigan Notre Dame football game—an incredible game. Michigan came back to win. The lead changed two or three times in the last few minutes. There were three touchdowns made in the last two minutes of the game. I turned off the TV and went to sleep.

Sunday, September 11

Since I had signed up for a floating trip on the Colorado River the day before, I had to get up at 6:00 a.m. We gathered in Page, where they had their office and where we boarded the buses. We left at 7:30 a.m. We were driven down to the other side of the dam where the Colorado River starts. About twenty of us loaded up onto this hard rubber pontoon. One could sit on the pontoon or on other seats on the inside. We had a guide that navigated us down the river and gave us great insight about interesting points along the way. The trip was about fifteen miles and took about three hours. The average speed was about four to five miles per hour. We did stop for about one hour to look at some images over five thousand years old carved on the stones. I did find a really cool stick from the Colorado River. I was very tempted to bring it with me, but there was a very tough female park ranger who might have seen it. And I didn't want to take the chance. As it turns out, I could have gotten away with it.

The water temperature was about forty-five degrees. I was tempted to go into the water. I went about knee-deep. There was a mix of people on our boat—mostly from Germany. One of the most interesting sights was a place called Horseshoe Bend. It had the shape of a horseshoe in the river. The boat landed at a place where other people took off from to go on a two- or three-week rafting trip on the Colorado River that took them through parts of the Grand Canyon. It was a long bus trip back to where we started in Page. I went to my car and took out a bottle of beer. After that, I also stopped on the way back to buy one more bottle of wine. That brought me back to the resort about 1:00 p.m., and I had some lunch and continued writing in my journal.

It is now about 4:00 p.m. The weather is overcast. It is way too early to call it a day. We have had a few short rain showers, but nothing to interrupt any activities until now.

A little preview about Monday and Tuesday—I booked through two days with a fishing guide. We are scheduled to start at 5:30 a.m. each day. I was planning to go to another beach nearby, but it got too late. Perhaps on Monday or Tuesday, if the weather permits. I retired to my room and watched Sunday Night Football.

Monday, September 12

The day started with a wake-up call at 4:00 a.m. to meet with the fishing guide at 5:30 a.m. This was the first of two days of fishing on the lake. We both got there at the same time. The guide's name was Mike, a very rugged, good-looking man in his sixties. He backed his truck and trailer into the lake and prepared his boat for launching. He didn't have the trailer far enough into the water. So while he was on his boat, I offered to back the truck farther into the lake. I managed with NO problems. I drove the truck and trailer out of the water while Mike docked the boat. We headed out at 6:00 a.m., and it was still dark but getting light slowly. It was in the midfifties at that time but felt much colder.

His fishing boat was just that—a fishing boat. It was nothing fancy but had all the necessary equipment and a very powerful motor. We were traveling about thirty miles per hour. This part was a bit cold. When we got to the fishing area and slowed things down, it got better. We fished awhile. If we didn't catch anything, we moved to another spot. I took some incredible pictures of the full moon and the sunrise and the solid rock canyons that surrounded us. We did catch a few fish at the different places we stopped at. Mike caught some, and I caught some. He caught more than me. We released all of them. We went back to where the big cruise ships were docked, and there was some large carp, striped bass, and catfish. We had a good time catching a few of those before it was time to call it a day. It was about 11:30 a.m., and the weather had warmed up by then. I backed the truck and trailer into the water so Mike could put the boat on it and then I pulled the boat and the trailer out of the water. I drank two beers while we were fishing. When I got back to my room I had a sandwich and some wine, watched some TV, and fell asleep.

I woke up at about 2:00 p.m. The weather had turned bad with rain and lightning. At 2:30 p.m., I heard a knock on my door. It was the girl I met on the beach. I told her to come back in five minutes so I could get dressed. When she did, we drove in to Page. She had to do some shopping. We went into one shop where I spotted an incredible brown leather belt that had beautiful hand-beaded designs in it made by Indians and a matching belt buckle. I wasn't really looking for anything, but when I saw that, I bought it. She bought herself a few things, and we headed back.

She knew of another beach on the lake that was bigger. The beach was named Lone Rock Beach because there is a HUGE rock formation in the middle of the lake. The weather had cleared up now. We walked around quite a bit. She collects different-sized rocks with interesting markings. She takes them back to her home in Tucson, Arizona, and sells them. We took some pictures. By now it was about 7:00 p.m., and we were getting hungry. So we went back to one of Page's better restaurants. It was an Italian restaurant—very simple and very popular. We had a nice dinner. I took her back to where she lives and said good night. I drove back to my place and watched some football and got caught up with my journal.

Tuesday, September 13

As usual, the day started very early—at 4:30 a.m.—to go on my second fishing trip. Little did I know at the time it was going to end up being a twenty-four-hour day. This time, I was better prepared for the weather. I met Mike at the boat ramp at 5:30

a.m. and helped him launch the boat. This time, we boated to a different part of the lake, about forty-five minutes away. After we slowed down to fish, it felt better and the sun was coming up. We moved around often enough but didn't have much luck this day. So we went back to the docks where the cruise ships were. This was a sure thing. The first fish was an eight-pound carp. It put up a good fight, then it was released it. We fished for an extra hour. He didn't charge me for the hour. Again I backed the truck and trailer into the water so he could put the boat in the trailer. Then I drove the truck up the ramp.

I told you there was more about the girl I met on the beach. Well, here goes. Right after I finished fishing, I was called by the girl I met on the beach. She asked if I wanted to go on a scenic drive with her to Mesquite, Nevada. Since I had nothing else to do, I agreed. Mesquite is just across the state line to Nevada. This was where it started to get interesting. Shortly after we started, we passed a guy hitchhiking. She told me to stop to pick him up, so I did. This was his lucky day. As it turns out he has (1) a prosthetic leg, (2) is an ex–Navy Seal, and (3) he was robbed of all his belongings that were very valuable. He was from New Orleans and was a very intelligent man.

As it turns out, the lady had a relative that lived in a small town that is on our way. So we stopped, and she talked to him and his wife and explained his circumstances. They were most generous. Bottom line was, they let him spend the night in a vacant trailer, gave him a sleeping bag, some kind of tarp, a very good hunting knife, and an old army bag to put it all in. The man we talked to had all kinds of junk he had collected. After talking to them for longer than we should have, we went on our way.

We headed out and went through Zion National Park. Shortly after entering the park, we saw several cars parked along the way. So we stopped also to see what they were looking at. There were several long-horned mountain goats about thirty feet above us on a very narrow ledge. We took some pictures. I found a walking stick, and we drove on.

The scenery was breathtaking. It started to rain a little. This was OK because there were several waterfalls that were created and added to the scenery. The road was very winding, so it took quite some time to drive through the park. After that, the drive to Mesquite was much quicker. By this time it was 8:00 p.m. There was a hotel casino with a gourmet restaurant in it. That's what I was hoping for. We had a gourmet dinner with a good bottle of red wine. After dinner, we went into the casino wear SHE played a cad game and then played some craps. We headed out. It must have been after midnight by then. It took us about three hours to get back.

It was after 3:00 a.m. by the time I got back to my room—just enough time for me to pack and go to the airport. I got there and checked in. The plane left at 6:30 a.m. It had now been well over twenty-four hours. When I got to Phoenix, I had a long time before my flight to Houston. That's when I finished writing about the long day. I had time for some breakfast as well. I boarded the flight to Houston and fell asleep. I arrived in Houston and was picked up by my friend Moe.

Trip to Costa Rica
Wednesday, November 23 to
Sunday, November 27, 2011

Wednesday, November 23

I was taken to the airport by Ron. Left the apartment at 6:30 a.m., and it was a good thing. Got to the airport and went through the check-in line and then the security line. Got to my gate with only ten minutes to spare. They were already starting to board the plane. When I made my reservation and used my one pass point for the dates I was traveling, it didn't cost me anything. On top of that, my flight to Panama was on first class. So I took advantage of that. Before we took off, we were asked what we would like to drink, so I had a Baileys and coffee. We did not take off on schedule because of some mechanical problem. We finally took off about forty-five minutes late. When we were airborne, the flight attendant took our breakfast order. The choice was an omelet or French toast. I chose the omelet. The flight to Panama took three hours. I had a glass of white wine since they didn't have champagne (bummer). The movie they were showing was *Rise of the Planet of the Apes*. I did get over keeping my elbows in while eating since I was in first class.

We did arrive in Panama about twenty-five minutes later than scheduled. I had just enough time to have a quick beer and make my connecting flight to San Jose, Costa Rica. The flight to Costa Rica took one hour. There was a snack and a beverage served on the flight. The temperature in Panama was eighty-nine degrees and overcast. I did finally sleep for a short time.

We landed in CR. It was very overcast, and it looked like it had rained earlier. Took a cab to the hotel. Got checked in and asked about fishing and scuba diving. To my disappointment, I found out that to do the diving would have taken much too long to get to. I went to a travel agency at the hotel to try to get me hooked up with a fishing charter. He made some calls, so I went out for the usual essentials (you know what they are). Also, I went to a bank to get money changed. I went back to the travel agent. He did not have any luck getting me on a fishing boat. By this time, it was after 7:30 p.m. I went up to my room and had very good dinner with the things I bought to eat and drink. I watched some TV and went to sleep.

Thursday, November 24, Thanksgiving Day

Woke up about 6:00 a.m. The weather was still very cloudy. I was lying in bed and tuned in to the Thanksgiving Parade. At about 10:30 a.m., I could hear some drums playing, so I looked out of my window. There in the park was a band competition made up of elementary-school-aged kids. I took some pictures and went on my way. Mostly just walking around. When I got back to the place where it all started, the winning band was just announced and was awarded a trophy. They were still all pumped up, banging on their instruments. I asked the bandleader if I could get into the middle of them and started playing the drums with them. I did catch on to their beat and kept up with them. I think they also had some fun with me. Had to have some pictures taken of this. After that, I went back to my room and had some snacks and watched some TV.

Around 7:00 p.m., I went to a nearby restaurant that featured a Thanksgiving dinner. After that, I went to a hotel very well-known for their "hospitality." The Hotel Del Rey was very small and offered a lounge, casino, and a restaurant bar with TVs. I went there and took advantage of their "hospitality." After that, I was feeling lucky, so I went to the casino and lost about $100. My hotel was only about two blocks away.

Friday, November 25

I have signed up for a white-water rafting trip on a river that is classified as a level 4, level 5 being the highest. SO I left a wake-up call for 6:00 a.m. Got down to the lobby at 6:30, the time that I was supposed to be picked up. The van finally came at shortly after 7:00 a.m. From the van, we were transferred to a bus. We drove for over three hours. We stopped for breakfast for a short time. We finally made it to our drop-off place. There was a long delay in letting us go through the gate because the president of the country was visiting that site where they intend to build a dam.

When we were allowed to proceed and get off the bus, we teamed up in groups of six. Our guide gave us some very complete instructions about rowing, when to row, when to stop rowing, and so on. Then we got into the rafts. Out of six people, there were five from Texas—four men and two women in total.

The first five hundred yards were the roughest and the most exciting. We didn't lose anyone. I learned later that a raft did lose someone. The guide was so experienced that he was able to pick HER up with no problem. It said on the brochure what we needed to wear and bring. I was prepared. It actually was raining at the time we were rafting, but it didn't matter because we were all wet anyway, and it wasn't cold. There were several other spots along the way that were level 4. At one point of our rafting, we were asked if anyone would like to get out of the raft and float on the water ahead of the raft. So I did because I have done it before.

One of the other crew took a great picture of me. I hope they will send it to me. After we got out of the raft, I found my walking stick along the banks of the river. We were told that the world championship for rafting was held on this river. We were picked up. We were driven to a place where we could shower and change. We all felt much better after that. Everyone was ready for lunch.

Trip to Winter Park, Colorado NASTAR National Championships (By Invitation Only) March 22 to March 25, 2012

Because I was at the Squaw Valley Ski Resort at Lake Tahoe, California, in February and entered the NASTAR downhill race and because of my age and my time that I finished, I won gold. A few weeks later, I received an invitation to attend the national championships. So I got right on it and made airline and hotel reservations. There were only a few weeks before they started. I was lucky to get a place at the Winter Park Mountain Lodge just across the street from the village where everything was taking place. I was there from Tuesday, March 20, and left on Monday, March 26.

Tuesday, March 20

Was taken to the airport by Ron very early in the morning. My flight was scheduled to leave at 8:45 a.m. Because of severe weather conditions, the airplane finally left Houston about at least three hours later. I arrived in Denver at about 2:00 p.m. instead of 10:30 a.m. Got the shuttle for WP at 3:00 p.m. Got to the WP Mountain Lodge close to 5:00 p.m. and checked in. I thought this would put me behind schedule, but luckily, they had a ski rental shop at the lodge. So I rented my boots, skis, and poles that day. I got that out of the way. Then I went out exploring and located some key places. I also got three important things out of the way: a cap from WP, a WP sew-on patch, and a stick to bring back to make into a walking cane.

While in the town of WP, I found a very good restaurant by the name of Deno's Mountain Bistro. It was an upscale sports bar and restaurant with a very good menu and wine list! This was where I ate almost all my dinners. The help got to know me very well. I had a usual high top table to sit at. The ski parka I wore all the time was bright yellow with sew-on patches from all over the world and United States and my cowboy hat that I wore while skiing. They both were very popular as you will find out soon. This very first night, for starters, while at the restaurant having dinner and a bottle of wine and writing the first of my daily journal, a group of young adults were looking at my parka and hat. One of the guys came over and asked me about the jacket. I told him about the patches. He then asked me if he could try it on. I said yes and he had to put the hat on also. Then one of the ladies wanted to try the hat on. Someone took a picture of the three of us. They promised to send me a picture of us all. Went back to the lodge, watched some TV, and went to sleep.

Wednesday, March 21

Got up at about 7:30 a.m., slowly got dressed, and went to get officially registered for the NASTAR race. There were a lot of forms to fill out and to sign. After that was done, I went over to the next table where I was given a lot of really neat things. The package included a great backpack and lots of coupons for ski stuff, a WP sew-on patch, a NASTAR medal with a red, white, and blue ribbon attached, two knitted NASTAR ski caps, a NASTAR lanyard, my own racing bib with my race number 1070, and a few more things.

I then found out my racing dates and times and places. My first race was at 9:30, Friday, the twenty-third. We all get two runs on both days. My second race day and time was Saturday, the twenty-fourth, at 12:30. Since Thursday, the twenty-second, was free, I will put my skis on for the first time and make a few runs. So after getting registered, I took a chairlift up the mountain to a lodge called Sunspot where they served food and drinks. I spent a lot of time there also. After I finished lunch and some wine about one and a half hours later, I took the lift back down to the village. I then caught the shuttle bus back to my lodge, took a shower, watched some TV, and dozed off for a while. Woke up, got dressed, and went back out about 7:30 p.m. to my favorite restaurant to write about this day. Had a very good bottle of white Burgundy and dinner.

Thursday, March 22

My first attempt at skiing. Got up about 7:30 a.m. It took me over an hour to put everything on. The ski boots were the toughest hurdle to overcome. It felt good to get a few runs in, and my skiing felt good as well. About noon, I skied to the Lodge at Sunspot for a well-deserved beer and a shot of tequila. Got back on the slopes and found some new runs. Stopped at the Sunspot and had a salad for lunch and a beer outside at a table. The weather the whole time I was there was beautiful. I was sitting next to a large post that had a ski parka, helmet, sunglasses, and gloves coming out of the sleeves. Of course I had my yellow parka and cowboy hat on (that I wore every day). There was a lady that approached me and asked if I wouldn't mind posing with her make-believe person (the made-up post). So I did. Everyone around who was watching had some good laughs. It was fun.

After my undisturbed lunch, I skied down the mountain. Put my skis and boots away (what a relief to take the boots off), and I went back to the village where the NASTAR activities were taking place and a stage with a rock band was playing. Just before that, I stopped someone who also was taking part in the races and asked him some questions. Of all the people I should run into at that exact moment, place, and time, it was none other than my cousin Richard Brooks. Talk about a one in a million chance.

Later we got together for dinner at a place he recommended. He was with two of his friends he goes skiing with all the time. The restaurant was OK; nothing special and too fancy. After I left there, I went across the road to my favorite place and had a slice of apple pie and a coffee drink. Made it to the bus stop just before they stopped running. Got back to my room and turned in.

Friday, March 23

Finally, it was time to race. So I got up early and without any hesitation this time, got dressed, and made it to my designated place to race just before 9:30 a.m. It took about one hour before it was my turn to race. It's very exciting when you're actually standing at the starting gate. My thoughts were making it down the course without falling or missing a gate. I did make it down without messing up. My time however was not very good: 53.62 seconds.

Made it back up the mountain for my second run. There was another long wait in line till all the first timers had their chance to race. Then we got in line for our second run. I got up to the starting gate. It was my turn to go. I started out very well, and it felt very good. About halfway down, for some unknown reason, I lost control and went off course. So I was given a DNF (did not finish). So I skied the rest of the way to Sunspot for a beer and a shot.

After about two hours, I skied the rest of the way down. Got to my room and took off my boots. Made myself a drink from what I brought from Houston. Went back to the stage area in the village. Had a slice of pizza and a bowl of soup. It must have been about 3:00 p.m. by now. All of a sudden, I spotted none other than Bruce Willis himself (I kid you not). I got a picture taken with him and another picture of him without his shirt on. He was with a small group of people. Then I also got him to sign my jacket. While sitting in the area, a married couple came up to me and admired my ski jacket and hat, and of course, took some more pictures.

There was a raffle for some prizes. I didn't win a raffle, but there were some celebrities there from the Winter Olympics from past years and the USA ski team. Picabo Street won gold in super G downhill at the 1998 Winter Olympcs. Heidi Voelker ranked in top five in the women's giant slalom. A. J. Kitt won gold in Downhill World Cup 1992. Ted Ligety won gold in 2006 men's super G. I got all their autographs on my jacket and my picture taken with them. Again, a couple came up to me that was admiring my jacket and hat, so I let the woman put them on to have some pictures taken. After all that was over, I took the shuttle into WP Town and had a good dinner with a good bottle of white Burgundy and then went back to my room.

Saturday, March 24

Today my time to race was 12:30 p.m. So far the weather has been sunny. Just below freezing in the morning and warmed up to the fifties during the day. Since my start time today was 12:30 p.m., I got up at 10:30 a.m. and got to the course at twelve noon. We switched race courses from the day before. It was time for my first run. I made it down in 41.34 seconds, ten seconds faster than my run on Friday. It really felt good. My second run was awful—49 seconds. I remember saying to myself while going down on both times, *You can make it. Just don't fall. Concentrate on the next gate.* After my second run, I skied to the Sunspot Lodge and had a beer and a shot. Now there was a man and his girlfriend that took a liking to me, and he took some pictures of me racing. We met at the lodge. We talked for a while. He bought me another beer and a shot (like I really needed that—NOT). He said he would e-mail me the picture and he did. By now it was about 3:30 p.m. I skied down the hill and checked my rental equipment in, put my after-ski boots on, and went back to the stage where everything was happening. I got the lead singer and guitar player's autographs on my jacket. I'm not sure who they were but so what. The Olympic ski team began announcing the winners of medals in the different groups. My name wasn't called, but I had a lot of fun!

Later I met up with Richard and his friends and went to Deno's for dinner. We ordered a second bottle of wine and then split the check four ways. Came to find out that my friend took care of the first bottle of wine. Oh yes, I had left my CC at the lodge, so when I got back to my lodge, we called the bar. They said they would keep it for me. So I went back on Sunday to get it. Richard drove me back to my lodge after dinner.

Sunday, March 25

Got up about 7:30 a.m. and finished writing about Saturday. Now it's 8:30a m. I got dressed and went out to get some things I needed. First I went to the photo place to pick out the best of my downhill racing pictures. It was hard to do; there were so many good ones—NOT. I picked out three of them. The man said they would be ready in thirty minutes. Then I found a road map of Colorado, so I could point out where WP was in relation to Denver. Then I went up the chairlift that took me to Sunspot Lodge where I left my CC the day before. They kept it and locked it up for me. When I got there, I decided to have a hot spiced wine just to pass some time, you understand. After that, I went back down to claim my pictures. The last thing was to get the exact names of the celebrities that were up here. When I got back to Houston, I looked them up and what each one was famous for to put into my journal.

I went back to my room and packed all the things. Now it was about noon. Took the shuttle back down to the base of the village where they were holding the final downhill races for those who qualified first, second, and third in their groups. I watched for a little while. Then I went to the place where they served lunch. I had a bowl of white curry chicken vegetable soup. It was very good. I sat there for a long time, watching the people. Because it was very warm at that time, the people were beginning to peel off layers of clothing. The WP ski area was very handicap friendly. I sat there until about 4:30. Went back to my room, got dressed for the nighttime, and took the shuttle to my favorite eating place. Had dinner and finished writing about today. Went back to my room and finished packing.

Monday, March 26

My plane back to Houston was scheduled to leave at 5:00 p.m. So the shuttle to drive me back to the Denver International Airport arrived at the lodge at 12:30. I got to the airport by about 3:00 p.m.—plenty of time to get checked in and go through security. I had a nice lunch at the airport before boarding the plane. When we left Denver, there were some very high winds, so the first part of the flight was a little bumpy. After that it was smooth. My friend Moe picked me up at the airport as usual. It was good to be home. Overall it was a great trip.

Autographs from baseball players and coaches on the active baseball roster and other baseball stars on my baseball tour, June 11 through September 4, 2012:

1. Oakland Athletics
    a. #4 Coco Crisp
    b. #15 Seth Smith
    c. #50 Grant Balfour
    d. #16 Josh Reddick (outfielder)
    e. #28 Eric Sogard (infielder)

f. #54 Travis Blackley (pitcher)
   g. #23 Chris Carter (outfielder)
   h. #38 Andrew Carignan (pitcher)
2. Fernando Valenzuela—retired Los Angeles Dodgers pitcher, rookie of the year, and pitched in the 1981 World Series
3. Los Angeles Dodgers
   a. #10 Tony Gwynn Jr.
   b. #21 Ted Lilly
   c. #22 Clayton Kershaw
4. Boston Red Sox
   a. #7 Cody Ross
5. Jeff Montgomery—retired relief pitcher for Kansas City Royals
6. Rollie Fingers—Hall of Fame pitcher, also with Kansas City
7. All-Star Game
   a. Ryan Cook (pitcher, Oak Athletics)
   b. Bryce Harper (outfielder, Washington Nationals)
8. Chris Berman and Buster Olney from ESPN
9. Arizona Diamondbacks pitchers
   a. #17 Trevor Bauer
   b. #29 Brad Ziegler
10. Minnesota Twins pitchers
    a. #39 P. J. Walters
    b. #58 Scott Diamond
    c. #50 Kameron Loe
11. Cleveland Indians
    a. #48 Travis Hafner (designated hitter)
12. Rick Dempsey, 1983 World Series MVP
13. Atlanta Braves
    a. Ryan Klesko (retired)
    b. Rob Belloir (retired)
14. Philadelphia Phillies
    a. #24 Ty Wigginton

15. Los Angeles Angels of Anaheim
    a. #18 Andrew Romine (infielder)
    b. #65 Nate Jones
    c. #43 Garrett Richards
16. Mark Salas—one of my favorites; bullpen catcher of the Chicago White Sox
17. Baltimore Orioles
    a. #10 Adam Jones (pitcher)
    b. #11 Robert Andino (infielder)
18. Washington Nationals
    a. #47 Gio Gonzalez (pitcher)
    b. #25 Adam LaRoche (baseman)
    c. #89 Joe Martinez (b p pitcher Wash Nats)
19. Pittsburgh Pirates
    a. #27 Jeff Karstens (starting pitcher)
20. Tampa Bay Rays
    a. #53 Alex Cobb (pitcher)
    b. #56 Fernando Rodney (pitcher)
    c. #9 Elliot Johnson
21. New York Mets
    a. #29 Ike Davis (first baseman)
    b. #44 Jason Bay
    c. #12 Scott Hairston
    d. #33 Mat Harvey (pitcher)
22. New York Yankees
    a. #14 Curtis Granderson
    b. #48 Jim Hickey (pitching coach)
    c. #19 Chris Stewart (catcher)

There are forty-nine autographs plus other celebrities not mentioned. The baseball trip only with list of number of autographs from trip.

Ronnie Bermann's Baseball Tour
June 11 to September 4, 2012

I started planning three months earlier with the help of AAA for the hotel. I did the rest with the baseball and airlines and sometimes train schedules. It actually started with the Astros and the Rangers, the two teams in Texas, starting in the last part of April to get them out of the way before actually starting to travel. In the first game of Astros versus LA Dodgers, Astros won 12–0 with a grand-slam home run. I parked for free and bought a $5 ticket and a beer for $7. Total cost was $12. I sat in the field box seats behind third base. I flew to Dallas, Texas, to see the Rangers in Arlington on Monday, May 14. The Rangers were playing versus Kansas City Royals.

My flight out of Houston was delayed over four hours. When I got to Dallas, I had just enough time go to the hotel right next to the stadium. I didn't make a reservation but asked if they had a room available. They didn't, so I left my one bag there and walked to the game. Bought a beer and sat down thirteen rows behind third base. In this trip, everything just fell into place as you will see. Two guys came and sat down beside me. They told me that they had the four seats but since there were only the two of them I could stay. So I bought them each a beer. I thought that was a good idea.

The Rangers star player, Hamilton, got a hit, but when he swung the bat, it flew out of his hands and into the crowd. This also happened to him the next time at bat. By the seventh inning, the Rangers had a comfortable lead, so I walked back to the hotel. I asked the manager if there was a room available now. She said she would check on it and let me know. So I went to the restaurant and sat at the bar. Asked the bartender for a menu. The bartender informed me that I was the last one to get the full menu. I was hungry, so I ordered the veal chop and a glass of red wine. I think it was a good thing that I ordered what I did (to be explained).

Shortly after I was served, the manager came back and told me there was a room. The bartender told me if I had ordered something like wings and iced tea, I probably wouldn't have gotten a room. I think he was kidding, but maybe not. After my second glass of wine, I jokingly said I would sell a ranch for a cigar. The man sitting next to me told me there were two men sitting outside where you could smoke that had three cigars (P. 2) on their table. So I went outside and asked if I could buy one of theirs. They told me to take any one I wanted at no charge. I sat down next to them and ordered a single malt scotch on the rocks with my cigar. What a treat! I remarked that if the rest of my trip was anything like this, I couldn't stand it. I flew back the next day.

Monday, June 11

I started my three-month trip. First stop was Denver, Colorado, to see the Rockies versus Oakland A's. I left Houston at 6:55 p.m. The temperature in Denver was between fifty-five to eighty-one degrees. I arrived in Denver about 9:00 p.m. Took a shuttle to the hotel that was in walking distance of the ballpark. Just before I left that day, I made two corrections. I checked in to the hotel and unpacked a bit. I did pack some vodka, Crown Royal, and some tequila. I noticed that one of the bottles leaked a little. No harm done. I just let the clothes dry. I had a few days in Denver. There was a liquor store two blocks from the hotel, so I stocked up on some vodka, Sprite, cranberry juice, and some cigars. There was a bar and grill next door. I had some buffalo wings and some beer then sat outside with a cigar and talked to some of the locals. What a day!

Tuesday, June 12

Woke up about 6:30 a.m., got ready slowly, took care of some business, and started writing about all that had happened up to today. I brought the wings from the night before to the lobby of the hotel and had lunch. The things I bought from the liquor store are coming in handy. After lunch, I started walking toward downtown and the stadium. Just then, I got a call from Ron. He wanted me to go to a restaurant that he had worked at before called Bayou Bob's to say hello to one of the managers. She was there, and I said hello from Ron. She remembered him. I took some pictures with her. I sat at the bar talking to some of the customers. One of them was from Houston but lives in Denver now.

Finally, about 4:30 p.m., I headed over to the ballpark. They let you in about two hours before the game sometimes. I went down to the side of the dugout to watch batting practice. I was wearing my #17 Berkman Astros jersey that I will wear to all the games. I was very lucky and got three of the A's autographs: #4 Coco Crisp, #15 Seth Smith, and #50 Grant Balfour. Then I went to the first base side and got two more autographs from the Rockies, #17 Todd Helton and #41 Wil Nieves. When it was time for the game to start, I noticed there were a lot more seats on the third base side, so I headed over there and found a seat twenty-four rows up directly behind third base. The weather at game time was eighty-one degrees and dropped to seventy-eight degrees. Rockies scored four runs in the first inning then the A's scored six runs in the fifth inning. The score ended 8–5, A's. I did bring a flask with vodka and cranberry juice in my pants pocket. The cup with ice cost $4.50. I got two good servings during the game. I left the game about the eighth inning and found my way to Morton's the

Steakhouse and had a good dinner and some wine, of course. With a few wrong turns, I made it back to the hotel.

Wednesday, June 13

I'm down in the lobby, and it's about 8:30 a.m., and I'm writing about yesterday's adventures. There is nothing planned for today, but the day just started. I will call cousin Larry to confirm with him when I will be in the Baltimore area so we will spend some time together. I do leave for Phoenix, Arizona, on Thursday, the fourteenth, where I understand the weather has been in the hundreds plus. It is still in the seventies here.

It's about 11:30 a.m. now. I went back to the liquor store to pick up a four-pack of the small red wine bottles to go with my leftover veal chop and asparagus and blue cheese from Morton's. At about 2:00 p.m., I walked to the Sixteenth Street free bus and wound up at the visitors information booth. I talked to two guys there to try to find out what to do for the rest of the day. It was too late in the day to go on any tours. It was suggested to go to a very well-known pool hall nearby. It was also the favorite hangout of a very famous woman, a world champion pool player, who sometimes shows up there. Her nickname was Viper, but her real name is Melissa Little.

Before heading over there, I was able to talk to one of the guys out of his bright yellow cap with the initials *BID* (I don't know what it stands for) on it that only they could wear. I got to the pool hall about 3:30 p.m. There was no charge for a table until 6:00 p.m. I actually ended up staying there until 10:30 p.m. I did have a few drinks, some wine, and some food. There were a lot of young people, a few older ones, and a surprising amount of women. The famous pool lady never showed up. It was close to midnight when I left the pool hall.

My plane for Phoenix, Arizona, left at 6:45 a.m., so I had to be there at least one hour before. My shuttle picked me up at ten to 5:00 a.m. So I had a wake-up call for 4:00 a.m.—about four hours' sleep.

Thursday, June 14

I arrived in Phoenix about 9:30 a.m., took the shuttle to the hotel, got settled, and am writing in my journal. The game I was going to see was only on Monday, the eighteenth, and I was going to leave on the nineteenth. I'm sure I will find plenty to do for four days. I'm going to go out and do some shopping now. Went into the town of Tempe, about four or five miles from Phoenix, Arizona, by light rail. Here the light rail is very functional and doesn't interrupt anything. It was very well-located, not like in Houston. They had an outdoor mall with a lot of restaurants and shops. I bought four short-sleeved button-down shirts and a pair of colorful cloth material slip-on boat-style shoes. Had some lunch at a nice Mexican restaurant. Took the light rail back to the hotel, about four or five blocks from the hotel. I could take the light rail in the other direction straight to the ballpark.

Since I had four days to kill, I was going to find out what there was to do. I thought it best to rent a car during that time, and I was right. I went to the computer room and tried to use the computer to look up some possibilities, but it was no use. I went to the front desk and the lady was able to hook me up with all my requests with tubing on the Salt River for Friday, the fifteenth; horseback riding early morning on Saturday, the sixteenth, and later that day, rafting on the river. She also printed out directions to all the places.

The hotel shuttled me to the airport for the rental car. Drove back to the hotel and had some lunch. Later that day, I got directions to a nearby casino. Got there about 8:00 p.m. Walked around a bit before sitting down at a blackjack table. Shelled out $100 that took me three hours to lose. The gourmet restaurant was closed for remodeling, so I settled for the other restaurant that was open. It was quite good. I couldn't finish all my food, so I took it back to the hotel. It was after midnight when I got back to the hotel.

Friday, June 15

Having the directions made it easy for me. I had to make reservations in advance for the horseback riding and the rafting. They were on Saturday. After batting practice was over, I walked around the whole ballpark. I made sure I remembered the aisle number and made sure the lady who was checking for tickets remembered me also. On my way around the ballpark, I met two people that had on the Astros jersey, so I had a picture taken with them. By the time I got back around to my aisle, the game was ready to start. I went in without a problem. Sat down behind third base just thirty-one rows up from the field. The D-backs won 7–1. Aaron Hill, one of their star players, batted for the cycle (home run, triple, double, and a single). It's only the fifth time it had been done by the D-backs. There were some great plays on defense and some good hitting. After the game, I walked to a nice restaurant to eat then got back on the light rail for the hotel.

Tuesday, June 19

I was shuttled to the airport to catch my plane to San Diego, California. The weather in Phoenix was in the hundreds. The weather in San Diego was sixty-four degrees. What a nice change. I got the shuttle from the airport to the hotel. There were no rooms available when I arrived. I was a little too early, so I spent the time writing in my journal. The room was ready at 1:00 p.m. Went to my room, got settled, went back out to take care of three things I needed to do. First, I went to the ticket office at the ballpark to pick up my tickets for the game. It was one of the only two times I had to do that. Second on the list was to go to the bus station to get a ticket for Anaheim just outside of Los Angeles for my next game. It was a short bus ride. Third on my list was to get another piece of luggage as a carry-on. After watching some TV, I finished writing about this day. I also rode the trolley to a few places.

Wednesday, June 20

The game between the San Diego Padres and Texas Rangers was at 3:40 p.m. I didn't have anything to do until 1:00 p.m. when I will head to the game. Got there in plenty of time for batting practice, but this time, I wasn't lucky at all, not even a ball. Hope this was not to be a trend. The weather was in the midsixties to mideighties with clear skies. I noticed that this ballpark didn't have a rolled-up tarp on either side of the baselines like all the other parks have to roll out when it rains. I asked someone else about that, and they didn't know. Maybe there is just so little rain in San Diego? The Padres took the lead at 2–0 until the fifth, sixth, and seventh innings when the Rangers scored four runs. That was the final score: 4–0. Nothing outstanding happened during the game. The Rangers were able to steal five or six bases, including stealing the third base. The game was over a little before 7:00 p.m. As usual, I found a seat behind third base, thirty-three rows back. I walked back to a bar and restaurant named House of Blues where I had been the night before. They had a local group playing the night before but nothing tonight. I tried to find a restaurant I had been in the night before but couldn't find it, so I walked back to the hotel and snacked on some leftovers from the night before. Did some packing and got the necessary papers ready for the next day.

Thursday, June 21

Got up about 7:30 a.m., finished packing, and checked out. On the way walking to the bus station, I took care of some things I needed to do. At the bus station, I got caught up with my journal since I had plenty of time. My next game was in Anaheim, California, a suburb of Los Angeles. I arrived there about 1:30 p.m. Took a short cab ride to the hotel and checked in. I didn't realize at the time that Disneyland was there. I took the shuttle a few blocks from my hotel to the entrance of the park. There is an area called Downtown Disney that is different from Disneyland—without the rides and mostly shops, hotels, and restaurants with some live entertainment. This is what I had in mind.

I had a light lunch at the House of Blues because I hadn't eaten yet. I walked around a lot. It was between 4:00 to 5:00 p.m. now. I saw a stage where a Latino group was going to perform after 6:00 p.m. I had an urge for a cigar, so I was directed to a place that sold them. I can be out in the open and smoke. I lit up the cigar and was standing a little ways in front of the stage where the group was playing. Most of the time, there was about a ten-foot space from anyone around me. This was also some of the best people watching ever. There was a young woman, maybe in her thirties, who looked at me as she was walking toward me, and I was looking at her. She came up to me, and we started talking. She wrote my phone number down on her hand and said she would call me later and walked away. Not thinking fast enough, I should have told her to call me before she walked away to make sure she had my number correctly because when she wrote it down, it didn't look right. I didn't hear from her. Her name was Crystal. She was with her brothers and some friends. What a shame.

After I finished my cigar, I went to the ESPN Zone bar. Game five of the NBA finals was on. So I went in and watched the second half of the game. Now it was about 9:00 p.m., so I went to another restaurant named Ralph Brennan's Jazz Kitchen, a very New Orleans–type place. There were two men playing the piano at the same time and singing. They were very good and very funny. They had fun with the crowd there. By this time, I was hungry again. I had a bowl of gumbo and some sort of tasty fish—I'm not sure what it was—and a couple of glasses of white wine. I had to keep an eye on the time because the last shuttle back to the hotel was at 11:30 p.m. So I made it back in time.

Friday, June 22

It was about 7:00 a.m. when I finished writing about yesterday's adventures. The game I'm going to see tonight is the LA Dodgers versus the LA Angels at 7:05 p.m. I needed to do a few things before going to the game. So I got dressed in my Astros attire, went out, and got the things I needed to do done. I had lunch at a small but good Italian place. It was a beautiful day, so I sat outside. I asked the waitress if it was possible to get to the game by bus. She said yes and explained to me how easy it was to do and it was. I got to the ballpark very early. I thought there would be some places of interest around the park, but there were only some apartments and businesses. It was about 4:00 p.m. then, so I sat down at one of the restaurants there and waited. At about 4:30 p.m., I walked to the entrance. There was a radio booth set up outside the gate that was connected with ESPN. They were broadcasting sports news. While I was there, the famous LA Dodgers pitcher, Fernando Valenzuela, who was rookie of the year and pitched in the 1981 World Series, was there. So I went up to him and got his autograph. The general manager of the Angels was being interviewed, so I waited till he was finished and got his autograph also. Now it was about time for the gates to open at 5:00 p.m. I tried to go down to the field as usual, but they were very strict there and only let you go there if you had a ticket for that row. I was able to stand near the field much farther down. I was very lucky to get the autographs of #10 Tony Gwynn Jr. and #21 Ted Lilly, both for the Dodgers.

Now it was game time. I found a seat just to the left of third base and twenty-four rows back. The Dodgers was leading in the first inning with a three-run home run. The Angels made it a close game in the middle innings and went ahead to stay. Final score was Angels 8–5 over the Dodgers. Got the bus back toward the hotel. I found one restaurant open—Joe's Crab Shack. After I ate, I walked back to the hotel.

Saturday, June 23

Got up at 5:00 a.m. Finished packing and started on my trip to Oakland, California. The trip was in two phases: first was the bus to the train station then the train to Oakland. While I was waiting for the train to depart, I was getting caught up with my journal. There was a very attractive young lady who sat down on a seat next to me. She watched me as I was writing in my journal and asked me what I was writing about. This was the start of our conversation. Of course, we continued talking. She was in her early twenties and was almost finished with college. She sings opera and was involved with a marketing company. As it happened, we were taking the same train. She was getting off a few stops before me. The train trip took over five hours, so we talked about a lot of different things. This made the train ride pass a lot faster and a lot more enjoyable. We exchanged cards, and I had some pictures taken with her before she got off the train.

I took the train because I thought it was going to be more scenic, but it wasn't. Only a lot of vineyards and other crops. I was scheduled to go back to Los Angeles by train, but I canceled that when I got to the hotel and made a plane reservation instead.

This part of my trip I was joined up with the lady I have known from the Lake Tahoe area, Colleen. We arranged to meet at the hotel we were staying at in Alameda, California—that is between Oakland and San Francisco. It was about 7:30 p.m. when I got off the train and took a cab to the hotel. She arrived only a short time before me. We got settled and went to a nice Mexican restaurant that was close by. We turned in when we got back to the hotel.

Sunday, June 24

I'm taking this time to do a load of wash and get caught up with my journal. We will be going to the Oakland A's game in the afternoon. It was about 11:00 a.m., so we decided to have a Bloody

Mary and a light appetizer at the same Mexican restaurant we were at before then left for the game. Colleen drove us to catch a walk-on ferryboat that took us within walking distance of the ballpark. She did a lot of research on every place we were going, with detailed maps, etc., that came in very handy. But sometimes I made fun of her.

We got to the ballpark about twelve noon and did manage to get an autograph from the batting coach of the San Francisco Giants. Because this game was sold out, we went to our assigned seats. The game was a good one. It ended with a walk-off three-run HR with two outs and a 3–2 count on the batter who hadn't hit a HR yet—one of the most exciting ways to end a game We took the ferry back to her car and drove back to the hotel and changed to go out to eat with a couple that she knew. Got to their house, and they drove us to a well-known restaurant in the area. They specialized in seafood. It was very good. We drove back to the hotel about 9:30 p.m.

Monday, June 25

I got up at 6:30 a.m. and went down to the lobby to finish writing in my journal. Colleen slept a little longer and took some time to get ready. Because she did so much advanced planning, the trips we took went very smoothly. There was another ferry we had to take at 1:30 p.m. to get into San Francisco. We had plenty of time, so we drove back to a small restaurant nearby the ferry and had lunch. We left the car at the ferry parking lot. This was much better than trying to park near the ballpark. The ferry goes to the piers in San Francisco. We walked around and went into some shops there and made our way back toward the ballpark. The gates opened at 5:15 p.m. There was a real nice bar across the street from the park, so we stopped there and had a drink. It was 4:30 p.m. then.

At 5:00 p.m., we lined up to go into the park. Once inside, I went down to get as close as I could to the playing field as I could. The area the fans could stand in was limited. With patience, luck, position, and timing, I was able to get #22 Clayton Kershaw of the Dodgers to sign my jersey. Because the game was a sellout, we went to our assigned seats. The Giants got four runs in the first inning and three runs in the second inning. The Giants scored again later in the game. The final score was 8–0 Giants. The Giants pitcher threw a three hitter. Colleen told me that the ferry leaves promptly thirty minutes after the game was over to take us back to where the car was parked in Alameda. We made it back to the hotel about 11:30 p.m. and went to bed.

Tuesday, June 26

It's about 7:00 a.m. I got up and went down to the lobby to finish writing about the previous day. Today Colleen and I will drive through the wine country and visit some wineries and eat lunch at one of the recommended restaurants in the area. I'm not sure after that. I leave to go back to Los Angeles on Wednesday, June 27. The weather in San Francisco has been beautiful—in the fifties and seventies and clear. We started out just after 10:00 a.m. As usual, Colleen had five different maps and a bunch of directions, which was a very good thing and was a lot of help.

The first of four wineries was Trefethen. All the grounds and tasting rooms of all the wineries were kept like five-star resorts and were very well organized. When you go in, they give you a choice of what degree of tasting you want to have. Since Colleen was driving, I chose the tasting program that usually offered the most wines. At Trefethen, we were able to join an older couple who were well-known there and had been there often. The program I signed up for offered five wines. We ended up tasting seven wines. The lady serving us was very nice. Colleen once in a while had a small taste of wine from my glass. Remember, she was driving. I took a lot of pictures of all the places we went to.

We left there and went to Domaine Chandon a little ways up the road. I took the four sparkling wine tasting and ended up tasting five. After that, we went to a restaurant for lunch that was recommended to us called Mustards Grill, a very popular and a very good place. I had a cup of soup and an appetizer. Colleen had a sandwich. We left there and went to Grgich Hills Estate. I tasted three wines, one white and two reds. The fourth and last one was Beringer Vineyard. It was OK. Colleen made reservations at a five-star restaurant named Auberge, and it was indeed five-star. The view was spectacular. This was why I didn't eat so much at lunch. I went all out for our dinner. I ordered Crystal champagne and caviar to start with. There was a couple that came over to talk to us for no apparent reason. We took some pictures together. We left to go back to the hotel after 9:30 p.m. It took about one hour to get back to the hotel. We went to sleep right away.

Wednesday, June 27

Got up at 6:30 a.m. and packed. Went down to the lobby to have some juice and write in my journal about the previous day. Today I fly back to Los Angeles and go to the game on the twenty-eighth. I arrived in Los Angeles at 1:15 p.m. It took some time before I got my bags. While I was waiting for my bags, a very attractive and well-built black lady who I had been talking to that was also on the plane to Los Angeles came up to me. Because I had told her about my trip, she asked if I could send her some pictures of my trip. I took a shuttle to the hotel. It was about 3:30 p.m. After I got checked in, I went back out to buy some casual shoes because I had worn out the other pair from all the walking I did. The other thing I had to do was to mail the two wine glasses I took from the wineries. I didn't break them, so I mailed them back to Houston. I got to the post office just before it closed. I also restocked on some liquids. After returning to the hotel, I went out to eat. I ended up at a Korean restaurant. The waitress could hardly speak English. Because I was hungry, I stayed there and ordered. When I got back to the hotel, I was ready to turn in.

Thursday, June 28

I woke up at 6:30 a.m. and turned on the TV because they were finally going to rule on ObamaCare at 9:00 a.m. ET, 7:00 a.m. PT. After hearing the ruling, I took a chair outside my room and began writing in my journal. It's another beautiful day in Los Angeles. The game today is at 7:00 p.m. The people at the front desk were very helpful and gave me directions to get to the ballpark. I had to change buses about three times.

It was about 11:00 a.m. when I headed out for the ballpark. I had to walk up the hill to get to the ballpark. Once again, there was nothing of interest around the park. So I asked one of the security guards where there was a place to eat and drink something. He directed me back down the hill far from where we started.

It was about 1:30 p.m. So I was going to spend about four hours there. I sat down at a bar and ordered a beer. They brought me some chips and salsa, and a little bit later, I ordered some pork tacos and a side of guacamole. There was a man sitting on the barstool next to me. He started a conversation with me because I had on my baseball outfit. He asked me the typical questions. When I told him what I was doing, he was totally impressed and started introducing me to some of the staff. Another one of them was equally impressed and became my "agent" so to speak. He also gave me the hat he was wearing. He asked if I could have it signed by a player. After a while, his girlfriend came in and joined him. She was a full-bodied and beautiful lady. Of course I had to have my picture taken with her.

In the meantime, my number 1 fan introduced me to a man who actually played on an AAA minor league team and was very well-known in the Dodgers organization. He offered to drive me to the game. It was much better than walking. Now this is the disappointing thing about Dodger Stadium. The fans are not allowed to go down to the field unless they had a ticket for that section and row. So I didn't get any autographs that day. So I had no choice but to go to my seat. Also the food courts were nothing special. So far my least favorite park.

The Mets took the early lead. The Dodgers made it a close game in the middle innings, but the Mets won 3–2. I made it back to the Mexican restaurant where I was before and had something else to eat. I got a cab back to the hotel about 1:00 a.m. Because my plane for Seattle leaves Los Angeles at 6:30 a.m., the shuttle picked me up at 3:30 a.m. I left a wake-up call for 3:00 a.m. I got two hours' sleep.

Friday, June 29

As I mentioned, the day started at 3:00 a.m. Got to the airport, checked in, and boarded the plane. Landed in Oakland, transferred to the plane for Seattle, Washington, and caught up on some sleep. In Seattle, with the help of some very nice people, I was able to take the light rail and then take a bus that dropped me off two blocks from the hotel at a total cost of $10. A lot less than taking a cab. When I got to the hotel, the room wasn't ready yet, so I had some lunch at a close-by grill. Went back to the hotel and sat in the lobby and wrote in my journal about the previous day.

It's now about 3:30 p.m. The weather in Seattle is cool and overcast. I rested for about two hours. I did a load of wash. I had thoughts of going out later but changed my mind. I went back to the same grill and had a late-night dinner and went to bed.

Saturday, June 30

I've been up since 6:30 a.m. I caught up with my journal. It's now about 8:30 a.m. Time to get dressed and go out. I'm going to the game tonight. I understand there is a lot more to do around the ballpark this time. First thing I did was to go back to the Amtrak station to get credit for the unused train ticket. Before I did that, I was in the area of Chinatown. Since it was 11:00 a.m., I decided to have a bowl of wonton soup and a beer. There was so much soup, so I took half of it with me. Did the Amtrak thing and took the bus and light rail back to the hotel. Believe it or not, I was getting good at making my way around.

Walked to what is known as the Space Needle. It was built for the World's Fair in 1962. So they were celebrating their fiftieth year anniversary. Took a lot of pictures from the outside. I found out that you could have lunch at the revolving restaurant near the top. So I bought a ticket and put my name on the list to be seated. There was an hour's wait, so I went all the way to the top and walked around on the outside deck and took some more pictures. I was given a thing that vibrates in your hand when your table is ready. It did, so I went down one floor to the restaurant and had a nice lunch and a glass of wine. By the time I was finished, it was perfect timing to go to the game. I walked back to the hotel, changed into my Astros outfit, and took the shuttle to the ballpark. It was 5:30 p.m. now. I got in and went directly down to the field. It was Elvis sunglasses giveaway night, so I got one. I was able to grab a baseball from the field and got autographs from #7 Cody Ross of the Boston Red Sox, the starting right fielder. I found a seat between the first base and the home plate thirty-seven rows back. Seattle took the early lead. Boston tied it up in the next inning. The game went to extra innings. In the bottom of the eleventh inning, Seattle had men on the third and first with one out. The batter hit a sharp line drive to the right fielder. The man on third hustled back to the base to tag up and started for home. The throw was not a good one, so the runner was safe. Now I've seen two walk-off wins. I took the shuttle back to the hotel, went to my room, finished the leftover soup, and went to bed. What a day!

Sunday, July 1

Caught the shuttle for the airport. My next stop was St. Louis, Missouri. I arrived in St. Louis at 3:00 p.m. Now I started my trip going east and the time was three hours later. Got a shuttle to the hotel. It's now close to 5:00 p.m. Checked in, went to my room, put things away, and went down to the front desk and asked the lady a bunch of questions. My first stop was to a supermarket. Restocked on some things, took them back to my room, made myself a margarita, went down to the lobby, and got caught up with the last two days in my journal. The temperature here is ninety-eight degrees. It's 7:30 p.m., and I'm going out for dinner. I have Monday, the second, and Tuesday, the third, to take in the sights and part of Wednesday, July 4, before the game. I'm going out to eat shortly. I realized that my necklace made of shells from my diving trips was missing. I don't know when or where it happened. But I can have another one made when I get back to Houston. So far I've lost my iPhone, necklace, and a credit card, all of which are replaceable. On the plane trip to St. Louis, I caught up on some sleep. I've skipped around a bit. It's after 8:00 p.m., so I walked to a nice restaurant that was named after an ex–St. Louis ballplayer, but I forgot the name. I sat at the bar and had a good dinner. I got back to the hotel at 9:30 p.m. and turned in for the night.

Monday, July 2

A very busy day. Got some information about some sights and names of jazz places, etc. My first stop was the famous Gateway Arch, which is over 630 feet high. Walked around the museum area inside the arch. There was a huge amount of space at the bottom of the arch. Took a lot of pictures and then bought a ticket for the tram that takes you to the top. It was very narrow at the top. I took some more pictures and came back down. I also bought a ticket for a paddleboat ride on the Mississippi river. The boat left at 3:00 p.m. It lasted one hour. Both things were interesting, but

I wouldn't do them again. Got back to my room about 5:30 p.m. Left a wake-up call for 8:45 p.m. to go back out. I woke up at 7:30 p.m. so I got dressed and went out. I didn't realize it was so early. The hotel shuttled me to the jazz bar area that was also close to the ballpark. A man asked me if I wanted to buy a ticket for the game for $10, so I bought it and went to the game. I left the game in the seventh inning. The score was 7–2 St. Louis. Now it was 10:00 p.m. So I walked back to the jazz bar area. The first one I went to was Broadway Oyster Bar. It was nice but time to go to the next place. They had a band but not a jazz band. They were very good. The first place was too quiet with older people. This place was more to my liking. It was after 1:00 p.m. So I walked back to the hotel and crashed.

Tuesday, July 3

Got out of bed at 10:30 a.m. Went to the bank and then was shuttled to a Laundromat and started a load of wash. There were a few nice restaurants a block away, so between washing and drying, I ordered a Bloody Mary and got caught up with my journal. I'm not sure what I will do for the rest of the day. It's another hot day in the midnineties. Finished my wash and went back to my room and rested for two hours. Took the light rail to a place called Blueberry Hill. They have concerts there but not today. It was still too early to have anything to eat or drink, so I went to the movies. It was a comedy about two kids and a scout troop with some big name stars in it. It was 10:00 p.m., and I was ready to eat. The Blueberry Hill was also a restaurant, so I had dinner and caught the light rail back to the hotel and turned in.

Wednesday, July 4

I started the day catching up with my journal (this is a full-time job but needs to be done). There was a parade going to start soon, so I stopped writing and went to the parade. At about noon, I made my way to the arch where they were having an air show and skydiving exhibition. I started back toward the hotel and saw a bar that I had been in before so I stopped in. *This is where the fun really started.* I sat down next to a couple from Knoxville, Tennessee. The lady was crazy, cool, and a lot of fun. We talked for a long time about a lot of different things. I told them what I was doing. They were very big college football fans. She showed me the schedule of games on her iPhone and told me to choose a game I wanted to see in Knoxville.

I'm not kidding. There is a game on September 8, University of Tennessee versus Georgia State University. So I told them I would like to go to that game. They gave me their phone numbers and to stay in touch with them. It looked like my trip will be extended. There is a concert later today taking place under the arch, and I will meet up with them and watch some of the concert before going to the game. This means I will probably not get any autographs this time. This has been totally cool!

It was 4:00 p.m. now. I was in the hotel lobby catching up writing in my journal about the amazing events of the day. I will head down to the concert in a short time and hook up with them again. I changed into my Astros jersey and cap. Before I left the hotel, I called the girl. They were at a bar called Big Daddy's that was located in an area with one bar after another and cobblestone streets, which were only for pedestrians. I really wished Houston could create an area like this.

I met and had a drink with them before heading out. The concert started at 6:30 p.m. It happened to be a band from Tennessee of all places. The concert was free except for a fenced-off area with chairs that one could sit down on. People brought blankets and coolers and their own chairs all around the outside fenced-off area. More and more people were gathering, but hardly anyone went in the fenced-off area until much later. The second performing group was Heart, a very well-known female singer. This was about the time that my friends showed up. Plus, they brought with them two other beautiful young girls they had met at the bar. I was very glad I brought two flasks of beverages with me. One was vodka and cranberry juice, the other was margaritas, and some cigars. I found us some cups with ice, and we all had something to drink. I also showed the girls how to smoke cigars. It's good to be prepared.

I stayed longer than I planned to and got to the game at the seventh inning. Looking back, I probably should have stayed with them. After the game, I went back to a bar I had been to before and bought a T-shirt that had the name of the bar on the front and "Leave your attitude at home" on the back. I found a bar that was still serving food and had live music. The restaurant was called BB's Jazz, Blues and Soups. It was very good. I took a doggie bag with me. It will come in handy later on my train trip to Kansas City. By the time I got back to my room, it was about 2:00 a.m. or later. I had a wake-up call for 7:00 a.m.

Thursday, July 5

It's 7:00 a.m. and time to get going. Washed up and finished packing. My one large suitcase was getting fuller all the time and the bottom legs have broken off. When I get to KC, I will buy a new and bigger one. I took the complimentary shuttle from the hotel to the train station. I will be boarding the train for KC soon. I was writing in my journal before I got on the train. I boarded the train at 9:15 a.m. The conductor said because of the heat, we couldn't go the normal speed, and we could be one and a half hours late getting into KC. It was a long six-and-a-half-hour trip. I packed some leftovers and some beers and ate lunch on the train. Because it was so cold, I moved to another car. I did sleep a lot of the time. I found about one hour before we arrived that they had playing cards for sale. I bought a deck and will use them often. When I arrived in KC, I called the hotel, and they sent me a black Continental Town Car. The driver was very knowledgeable about the city and took me on a brief tour on the way to the hotel. The driver was very nice and the sightseeing tour was not extra. In fact,

I used him for all my transportation needs. I got to the hotel after 8:00 p.m. I had some more leftovers and a beer that I enjoyed in my room. Watched some TV and went to sleep.

Friday, July 6

Got up about 7:00 a.m. and got ready slowly. I called for my limo driver to take me to a Walmart. I bought a new suitcase, some more ankle-high socks, and a pint of vodka. This didn't take long. I called Jim (my driver), and he took me to the ballpark to pick up my three-day ALL-STAR package tickets. I was glad to get that out of the way! I also bought a one-day Fan Fair ticket. There was a bunch of different activities, exhibits, and shops.

I walked back to the hotel, which wasn't very far. Got to my room and changed into my Astros jersey and cap. It's about twelve noon, and I'm getting caught up with writing in my journal. I will go to the Fan Fair soon. What an unexpected day and evening it turned out to be.

I was driven to the Kansas City Convention Center where the fair was taking place. It was huge. My first stop was to the All-Star shop to buy an All-Star program, a KC All-Star cap, an All-Star hat pin, and a lanyard to put my three tickets in to wear around my neck.

I then looked at a map of activities that I would like to do and see. First was the batting cage where they videotape your swing and analyze it. They have my e-mail address and are supposed to send it to me. Next was trying to throw a baseball through a one-and-a-half-foot round hole from about six feet away. I threw the ball almost over the backboard.

It was about twelve noon, so I went to a concession stand and got something to eat. Next was a virtual batting cage. There was one wire connected to you and another connected to the bat. There was a screen with a man pitching a ball to you. So you had to time your swing to make contact with the ball. Each person got ten swings. I managed to hit two HRs. I had someone take a picture of me in the cage. I had my picture taken as if I were a pitcher on a pitcher's mound and one of me making a spectacular catch in the outfield.

Then there was a place where they made a baseball card of you striking a pose and swinging a bat with your name on it. My pose was like I had just hit a HR. Later I saw a man who was taking those pictures. He recognized me and told me mine was the best one of the day.

Then I went to watch a miniature-sized baseball game between some of the staff and some local celebrities. I saw a very attractive and well-built lady who used to work for the Astros but now worked for the Texas Rangers. I couldn't resist having my picture taken with her. There was also a bunting cage. So I gave that a try. I found out a very good retired relief pitcher for the KC Royals, Jeff Montgomery, was signing autographs. The line for him was not very long.

I went back where the Hall of Fame pitcher Raleigh Fingers, also a relief pitcher for KC, was and stood in line for two hours to get his autograph. On my way out, I bought an official Louisville Slugger All-Star bat with my name on it. It was 7:00 p.m. I had spent six hours there. I was told about a very good restaurant called the Majestic Restaurant about three or four blocks away. I got there about 8:00 p.m. and went downstairs where they had a live band and sat at the bar. I had a very good dinner and a nice bottle of wine. I took what I couldn't finish with me. Took a cab back to the hotel. I got a call from Ron at 2:30 a.m., but nothing was wrong. I slept till 9:30 a.m.

Saturday, July 7

Got up and started to do some laundry again. So I'm taking this time to write in my journal. There are a lot of kids here because of a water park connected to the hotel. I had some lunch with the leftovers from last night. I took my baseball bat and some other things and shipped them back to me. I messed around until 6:00 p.m. and went back out to the jazz bar district on 18th and Vine. There is also a negro baseball hall of fame museum here. I went to the museum first and walked around there for a long time. There was a lot of interesting things to see. There was some kind of charitable function going on with free food and wine and a band. I didn't eat anything but had some wine and listened to the band. I didn't eat anything because I was going to one of the best BBQ places in KC only five or six blocks down the street.

At about 8:00 p.m., I walked over there. I ordered a BBQ combo and some fries. It was too much to finish, so I took it with me. It's about 10:00 p.m. now, so I walked back to the jazz district. My first stop was called the Blues Room. There was a four-piece group with a trumpet player as the lead. They were good, but the place was too quiet. In fact someone called down some others that were making too much noise. I left after their first set and walked across the street to a place called Danny's Big Easy, a much better, noisier place. The other place was too jazzy. This place had a big band with four singers. The first place had a $10 cover; this place was only a $5 cover. I stayed there until 1:30 a.m. Then I got a ride back to the hotel.

Sunday, July 8

Got up around 10:00 a.m. Took my camera to a Walgreens to have some pictures developed and added some text to some of them. Got about fifteen of them printed and went back to the hotel and grabbed a bite to eat and a beer. Changed into my Astros jersey since the ballpark was just across the highway. I walked over. The first event was called the Futures Game with the new hopefuls from the minor leagues against each other. It was the USA versus the world. The other team consisted of players from other countries. I got there about one hour before the game and was able to get four or five autographs. The score ended 7–5 USA. The next event was the celebrity softball game, matching some celebrities in entertainment and some retired baseball players on each team. I did get the autographs of Eric Stonestreet (*Modern Family* and Emmy Award winner), Haley Reinhart (*American Idol*) James Denton (former *Desperate Housewives* star), and Chrissy Teigen (model). I was very lucky. It was a six-inning game and very entertaining. On the way back, I walked through some tailgaters, three guys, and of course, I asked for a beer. We talked for a long time. It was 10:30 p.m. now. I had a picture taken with them. I got back to the hotel and finished my leftovers and went to bed.

Monday, July 9

I got up about 10:00 a.m., made some phone calls, and came down to the lobby to catch up on the last two days. The only event today was the HR Derby that starts at 7:00 p.m. I will get there about 6:00 p.m. I spent most of the day at the hotel. Shortly before 5:00 p.m., I left the hotel for the ballpark. Walked in and went down to the playing field to do the usual. I got the autographs of Ryan Cook, pitcher, Oakland A's; Bryce Harper, OF, Washington Nationals; and a local TV personality, Miles.

There was a great CW band that played for the pregame, the Zac Brown Band. They were great! Now when they announced the participants for the Home Run Derby, in came to Robinson Canó, who was the winner of last year's Home Run Derby and he did the selection for the members for this year's HRD. They booed him so much it was impossible to hear the interview BECAUSE they were playing in KC and Canó didn't select Billy Butler from KC, one of their star players and should have been selected. In fact, when it was Canó's turn to bat, the fans booed him even louder and cheered when he didn't hit a HR. And even worse, he didn't hit a single one on his turn at the bat. Prince Fielder won the HRD from Detroit. After the HRD was over, I went back toward the playing field and got two more autographs—one from Buster Olney from ESPN and Chris Berman also from ESPN. Overall, a very good evening. As I walked back to my hotel, I stopped at the Taco Bell (the only thing open) and bought two tacos that I took back to the room to eat, and I went to bed.

Tuesday, July 10
The Day of the All-Star Game

The day started very badly with a call from my friend Moe. Because he was at my place on Monday to deliver some Tarima to a wine boutique for me. He had to go into my apartment to get it. So when he called me today and told me how bad the place looked, I called my brother, Mark, to ask him what I should do. He told me to fly back to Houston. So I made reservations to take a plane back to Houston early morning Wednesday, the eleventh, and take care of whatever I need to do at that time. I plan to take care of a lot of things and return to KC on Saturday, the fourteenth, afternoon in time to catch the regular KC game at 6:00 p.m. that evening.

Now back to today. I had lunch at the Majestic Restaurant that I had dinner at the other night. After lunch, I caught a cab back to the hotel and changed into my Astros outfit and walked to the ballpark. I got there at 5:00 p.m. The game started at 7:30 p.m. with the pregame stuff at 6:30 p.m. So batting practice was over much sooner. So this time I was not lucky and didn't get any autographs. So I went to my seat. The NL scored five runs in the first inning. The final score was 8–0 NL. As I walked back through the parking lot and I saw some tailgaters, I asked them for a beer and talked to them a while. I walked back to the hotel and got the leftovers from lunch and brought them down to the lounge area of the hotel. I got a wake-up call for 5:00 a.m.

Wednesday, July 11

Got up at 5:00 p.m. and gathered the things I needed for the short time I will be in Houston. I'm in the airport now waiting to board the plane and catching up with my journal. My trip back to Houston will not be a pleasant one. I need to see for myself what condition the apartment is in. I arrived in Houston at 10:30 a.m. My friend Moe picked me up and brought me to my place.

I went up to my place. Ron was sleeping on my bed. That was OK because I wasn't there. BUT the place was a complete mess. I woke Ron up and told him he needed to be out when I left on Saturday, the fourteenth, and I told him why. He was upset but didn't say much. I sorted out my mail, made some calls, paid some bills, and a few other things.

Thursday, July 12

I caught up on some sleep and didn't go out of the unit. This is also amazing. I called a lady that wants me to do a bartending job for her tomorrow to let her know I would be in town and was able to do the job. She was very pleased. I called Renee to help me as a server. The timing for my trip couldn't have been more perfect.

Friday, July 13

I called a locksmith to have new locks and keys made. I also picked up a good check from the people I did some catering for before I left on my trip. When I got home, I made out a check for Renee and went to bed.

Friday, July 14

I leave this morning for KC to see a game tonight. The timing for the three days couldn't have been any better. Moe picked me up at 9:15 a.m. to drive me back to the airport. I am getting caught up with my journal. Boarded the plane at 11:20 a.m. Arrived back in KC at 1:20 p.m. and arranged for transportation back to the hotel ahead of time. Everything in the room was just as I left it—a great relief.

I brought back a few more things that I would need for the next two months. After I got organized, I went down to the snack bar and had some lunch. It was about 12:30 p.m. now. Went back up to my room and rested for two hours. Changed into my baseball attire and walked to the game. This was one of the highlights of my trip. Went down to the seats just behind the Chicago White Sox dugout on the third-base side and managed to get two autographs. First was #38 Eduardo Escobar (utility infielder). The second, #59 Mark Salas, the bullpen catcher.

This was the most enjoyable and outrageous conversation we had. As usual you had to make eye contact with the player before you throw them anything. I did so, and I threw him my jersey and pen. He disappeared into the dugout for a while with my jersey and came back a short time later. "What do you want me to do with this fucking thing?" I replied, "Wear it if you want to." Everything he said was in fun (I think). The first thing he said to me after signing my jersey and throwing it back to me was "Don't you wear this jersey and cap in my stadium." I believed he was serious. What a great conversation. I will talk about it for a long time.

As usual, about thirty minutes before the game, the ushers cleared out the area except for the people who have tickets for that area. So I walked around the food courts, bought a beer, and just before or just after the game started, I found a good seat somewhere behind the third-base dugout. The game was a good one with three HRs, two triples, some great defensive plays, a stolen base, and a caught stealing. Most of the scoring was in the middle innings. It was a 3–3 tie. The Royals scored one in the seventh and two more in the eighth. Final score: Kansas City 6, White Sox 3.

The time was 9:30 p.m. Walked back to the hotel, went to my room, and brought the leftovers down to the bar area with a large cup of something to drink. The bar area at this hotel was very lively. There was group of people from Nebraska in the bar singing and carrying on. One of the men came over to me and asked me why I was there. After I told him, four or five more people came over and joined in the conversation. They live in Omaha, Nebraska, the home of the College World Series. So now I've been invited to come to Omaha for the College WS some time in June. So we exchanged cards. It might be fun to go. Went back to my room and left a wake-up call for 4:30 a.m.

Sunday, July 15

Got to the airport in plenty of time. This plane was a small one with only one seat on one side and two seats on the other instead of three seats on each side. I left KC with the weather in the nineties. Changed planes in Chicago in the seventies for my next destination, Cincinnati, Ohio. I arrived in Cincinnati about 11:30 a.m. I got the shuttle to my hotel. It was too far from the ballpark, so I got the yellow pages and found a Holiday Inn about one mile away. This was the only time I had to change hotels. I also found out there was a trolley one block away that picks you up and takes you to the game. I went to a liquor store one block away and restocked.

The front desk told me about a jazz club restaurant with live entertainment. I am going there tonight. On the way to the liquor store, I started a load of laundry. I was glad I switched hotels. I stayed in my hotel room and rested until 6:30 p.m. then walked to the jazz club named Chez Nora. It was on the third floor. Not so large of a place. The place was full. I did see an empty chair at a table with other people. So I asked if I could join them. They said yes but the chair I was sitting on was the seat that belonged to the piano player. They had just started again after taking a break, so I had some time before they would take another break.

In the meantime, one of the couples got up and left. So I was OK. It was a four-piece band and a singer. All of them were my age and older, except for the drummer. I did order some food and a bottle of wine. The people at the table were all very nice, and we had some good conversations about what I was doing. I found a postcard-sized paper with the name of the place, so I had the band members and the singer sign it. I also asked the drummer for a drumstick, and he gave me.

When they took a break, some of the people left. The band had one more set to do before they were finished for the night. Since there were empty chairs closer to the end, there were some people that moved in and sat down. I'm not sure how it came up, but the lady next to me went a little crazy when she heard French. So of course I started speaking French to her, and she did get excited. Her husband was sitting on the other side of me so I decided not to speak too much French (nothing had happened). I took the cheese with me to go.

On my way back, I passed another bar which was much more lively. They had a DJ, and there was dancing. Immediately as I walked in, I was sandwiched between two young ladies who were bumping and grinding on me. Smoking was permitted in the place, so I went quickly at the back of the hotel and returned with three cigars. I couldn't resist giving one of them to one of the ladies I was dancing with and proceeded to show her how to light it. Of course she knew what to do and did it much better. After a while I got bored with them and moved to another part of the bar and mixed with another group of people. Had some tequilas and walked back to the hotel at about 3:30 a.m. Another long but good day.

Monday, July 16

It's after 9:30 a.m. when I woke up. I went down to the breakfast room and had some orange juice, and I'm writing in my journal now. I plan on going back to the jazz club for lunch. The game this evening is at 7:10 p.m. I leave for Milwaukee, Wisconsin, on Tuesday, the seventeenth.

The baseball games were fun, but I was having more fun in between games. I caught the bus that takes you within one block on the ballpark. I got there at 4:30 p.m. and went to a bar for a glass of wine before going to the stadium. At 5:00 p.m., the gates opened. I walked down to the field. The D-backs were taking BP. It took some time before some of the players started heading our way. The passions and positions paid off. I was able to get the autographs of #17 Trevor Bauer, a pitcher, and #29 Brad Ziegler, also a pitcher. Both played for the D-backs.

Again I walked around until the start of the game then went down and found a seat on the first-base line between first base and the left field foul pole and was close to the playing field. The D-backs scored five runs in the first inning. The Reds scored three runs a few innings later. The D-backs scored one more run. D-backs won 6–3.

After the game ended, I walked to a new bar that had recently opened. This was when the fun started as I said before. I asked the guy I was sitting next to which bus to catch to get back to my hotel. He and three other friends were catching the same bus, and they lived very close to where you get off the bus. They invited me to join them at his house before walking back to the hotel. So I did. They opened some wine, and we had a choice of wine, beer, or other drinks. They also could find any music by connecting something to their stereo system. The place was very nice. They defrosted some chicken, and I was slicing and dicing tomatoes and onions. He lit up the grill outside, and before we knew it, we were eating chicken tacos and salsa.

The guy called another girl to come over. There were three guys, three girls, and me. I walked back to the hotel, which was not far away. I had no idea what time it was. But what a great experience! This was one of the three or four best parts of my trip.

Tuesday, July 17

I woke up at 6:30 a.m., packed, and went down to the breakfast room and had some juice and wrote in my journal before getting on the shuttle for the airport. I fly to Milwaukee, Wisconsin, today and go to the game on June 18. I got there about twelve noon. Took the shuttle to the hotel and did some organizing because I leave Milwaukee right after the game. I must not have done much that I can remember on the seventeenth.

Wednesday, July 18

The game between Milwaukee and St. Louis was at 1:10 p.m. Milwaukee won 4–2. I walked to a restaurant nearby because I hadn't eaten all day and was good and hungry. I got back to the hotel and retrieved my things and took the shuttle to the airport. My plane to Minneapolis-Saint Paul, Minnesota, left at 7:20 p.m. and got in at midnight. I called ahead to let them know and to hold my room. The game in Minneapolis was at twelve noon.

It's now June 19, and I'm caching up on two days of not writing in my journal. That's why things are so confused. I got to the hotel about 4:00 a.m. and slept a few hours. Got up and took the shuttle to the ballpark. I got to the ballpark at 10:30 a.m. The gates already opened, so I went down to the field. I found out that if an afternoon game followed a night game, there was no BP that day. The ballplayers were on their own to warm up. Some of the players came over on their own to sign autographs. I managed to get three: #39 P. J. Walters, a pitcher; #58 Scott Diamond, also a pitcher; and #50 Kameron Loe, another pitcher—all from the Twins.

It was a very beautiful and clear day. I was able to find a seat in the shade. There were three guys sitting behind me that noticed my jersey and autographs and began asking me a lot of questions during the course of the game. One of the guys was doing the same thing but in a much longer period and was only missing two parks in Florida. The ballpark was in the downtown area.

On the way to the ballpark, I passed a very nice Irish pub with a nice outside seating. The game was over at about 3:00 p.m., so I walked back to the pub. Since smoking was allowed outside, I found a cigar store and bought four cigars. It was about 5:00 p.m. now. I sat back down and ordered a glass of white wine.

Not too long after that, guess who should appear? Yes, the three guys I was talking to at the game. I motioned to them to join me. They ordered some beers. I asked if they smoked cigars. They said yes, so I gave them each a cigar, and they lit up. We talked about almost everything—work-related and otherwise. Mostly otherwise. I had my picture taken with the four of us. We parted ways a few drinks later. It was about 8:00 p.m. at this time. I walked to a seafood restaurant that I noticed before. It looked very nice with a good menu and equally good wine selection. I was given the option to sit outside, so I did. It was well after 10:00 p.m. when I finished. I asked which bus to take to get back to the hotel.

Friday, July 20

A day off to recuperate. I woke up at 7:00 a.m. and dozed off several times before getting out of bed. I slowly got ready went down to the lobby where I'm finally catching up with my journal after two days. It's almost 1:00 p.m. now, so I brought some of the leftovers from a few days ago that were still good and had lunch in the lobby. I also had some pictures developed and put some texts on some of them. I got quite a lot of them done. This took some time. It's time to go back downtown to some of the restaurants and bars that were recommended to me. Went to one pub, can't remember the name, and had a glass of wine. There was a large group of people there that were doing a pub walk (crawl) for a charity. Then went back to the Irish pub with outside seating. It's about 6:00 p.m., so I decided to go to the Capital Grille, a very well-known steak house. Enjoyed a very good dinner with a nice bottle of wine as usual. I couldn't finish it, so I took the food and the unfinished wine back to the room with me. It was about twelve midnight, and I packed everything.

Saturday, July 21

Got up at 6:00 a.m. and got to the airport at 6:45 a.m. The plane was supposed to leave at 9:40 a.m. but left at 10:20 a.m. Changed planes in Chicago for Cleveland. I had five minutes to catch the plane. So they held the plane for me and my bags. Arrived in Cleveland at 2:00 p.m. ECT. I took a train into the city and a cab to the hotel. Total cost: $7.50.

After I checked in to the hotel, I had received a voice mail from Larry Mayer because I intend to take a side trip and visit them when I get to Baltimore, Maryland. Baltimore is my next stop when I leave here. So I called him back and told him my schedule. We will work out the arrangements.

What happens next is a must read. I went to the ice machine to get some ice to make myself a drink. I put the bolt in front of the door so it wouldn't shut. When I came back, the door was still partially opened, so the lady that cleans the room saw the door and asked me if everything was OK. So I asked her to come in. We started talking. She was very friendly and quite personable. She had just gotten off work. So we had some intimate times together. I will most likely see her again before I leave. The game I'm going to is on Sunday, twenty-second, at 3:00 p.m. I leave on Monday, twenty-third.

Sunday, July 22

I actually spent the night with her on Saturday and was brought back to the hotel this morning at 10:00 a.m. I took a shower. Took some leftover food down to the lobby and had some lunch at 11:00 a.m. Went to the Rock and Roll Hall of Fame about six to seven blocks away. I spent one and a half hours there. Took some pictures, and bought a hat and a pin. It was very interesting.

Walked back to the hotel, changed into my Astros uniform, and walked to the game about six to seven blocks in the other direction. Had a beer at a bar close by. They opened the gates at 1:30 p.m. I waited until the lines had gone down before going in. Same as usual, went down to the field level. I did get the autographs of #29 Tommy Hunter, a pitcher for Baltimore, and #50 Miguel Gonzalez, also a pitcher for Baltimore, and he threw me a baseball. I now have three balls. I also have a ball from the All-Star game to add to my collection. Since I am collecting so many things, I will mail most of it back to myself. This was very necessary to keep my bags light and make room for more stuff. Was time to walk around the park before the game started and find a seat. I sat down thirty rows back of third base.

The game was OK. Baltimore scored first. The score was 4–0 until the ninth inning. Cleveland scored three runs. Final score, 4–3 Baltimore. I stayed around a little and finished my margarita that I brought into the game. If I didn't mention it, I usually brought something to drink into the game with me.

When I walked out of the ballpark, I accidentally walked past the area that the ballplayers came out after the game, so I got #48

Travis Hafner the designated hitter for Cleveland. Went back to the hotel and asked where there was a nice restaurant nearby. It was 7:30 p.m. now, and I was good and hungry. I went to one of the recommended restaurants and had a good dinner with a bottle of wine and took my time. I took the leftover food and wine back to the hotel. Leftovers have always come in handy.

Monday, July 23

Woke up at 6:30 a.m., packed, and checked out. The cab and train to the airport cost $9 total including tip. Got to the airport early and got to the gate with plenty of time to write in my journal. I forgot to mention the flags were at half-staff at the game on Sunday, twenty-second, because of the shooting in Colorado (when I wait over a day to write in my journal it's hard to remember all the details). So far I think I've remembered most everything.

I arrived in Baltimore at 12:30 p.m. Took the light rail and a cab to the hotel at the cost of only $7 including tip. I learned to save a lot of money traveling in cities and spent it elsewhere.

The hotel I was booked into was not in a convenient location this time. The lady at the front desk was very helpful and got me into one of their other properties, which was much closer to everything. It was too late to cancel, so I stayed there just for one night.

I spent the time very well. Went to the bank, did a load of wash, and sent over ten pounds of things that I collected and didn't need to carry with me back to Houston. I'm sure I will send back more things during my trip. It was after 8:30 p.m., so I was able to find a nice bar that was still open and had something to eat. It wasn't bad. That was all for Monday.

Tuesday, July 24

Had a good night's sleep. Got up at 8:30 a.m., went down to the breakfast room, and wrote in my journal. I moved to the other hotel that was much more convenient to the ballpark and the harbor. There are a lot of historical sites to see in Baltimore.

It's now 11:00 a.m., and I planned to spend the day at the harbor. It's very interesting and the second busiest harbor on the East Coast. First I took a forty-five-minute cruise around the harbor. The town of Baltimore did a lot of necessary cleaning up of the area around the harbor. On the cruise, we passed Fort McHenry where Francis Scott Key wrote the national anthem.

Next I went on a self-guided tour of the USS *Constellation*, a large sailing ship with cannons on both sides. It saw a lot of action between 1854 and 1893. I managed to take a belaying pin from the ship that I will have framed when I get back. I also took a self-guided tour of the WWII submarine USS *Torsk*. President Carter served on this boat.

Then I took the water taxi to where there was a ride on a pirate boat called *The Urban Pirate*. It was mostly for kids and their parents. It lasted one and a half hours but was fun anyway. There was a pirate cruise for adults where they play adult games. It was on the day after I would have left. It's now 5:30 p.m. and was time to eat. I went to a place where the locals go to eat. I had soft-shell crabs to start and crab cakes for my main course with a bottle of white Burgundy wine. After dinner, the restaurant shuttled me back to the hotel with no charge. I gave him a nice tip. Went to bed at 10:30 p.m. A very good day.

Wednesday, July 25

Today I will rent a car equipped with a GPS. That was the best investment I could have made. It was about 9:30 a.m. I called the

Enterprise Rent-a-Car to pick me up at the hotel at 10:30 a.m. I wrote as much as I could in my journal before they picked me up. I drove to Ocean View, Delaware, where Larry and Barbara Mayer lived and spent Wednesday and Thursday with them. I left Baltimore at 11:00 a.m. It took two and a half hours to get there with only one slight turnaround.

I got to their house at 1:30 p.m. Larry and Barbara were home because they were expecting me. They live in a two-story home in a very nice subdivision with two VERY BIG and friendly dogs. I had something small to eat. We had a long but very good conversation about a lot of things—one of many good conversations.

After I ate, Larry drove me all around the area. We drove along where there was some Atlantic Ocean beach coastline on one side. We got out and walked around a bit. I had to go into the water just because. On the other side was the bay. There were a lot of very expensive homes and a lot of cornfields and other crops.

Larry explained how and why they decided to buy a trotting horse, who by the way has won a good number of important races—in spite of the fact that they didn't pay very much for the horse. Also, he explained about the stables, the trainer, and the jockey and about some of the other correctors that were at the stables. The whole story could be made into a movie. It sounded very familiar. Taking care of the horse was a full-time job, but they seem to love it.

When Larry and I returned, it was time to walk the dogs. It was 5:00 p.m. now, so we went to a small but very nice Italian restaurant with good food. When we finished eating, it was 6:30 p.m.

Then we went to a trotting horse race. Larry and Barbara bet on almost all the races. They knew what to look for. They knew the jockeys (they are not called jockeys; they're called riders because they are not sitting on the horse), and they knew what to look for in a horse and their track records as well. We all had programs to look at. I bet on five races and didn't win anything. I think Barbara won $18. When we got back to the house, I took a shower and went to bed.

Thursday, July 26

We got up at 6:30 a.m. They had a little breakfast, and I had some coffee. We took the dogs for a short walk. Larry had an eye doctor appointment, so Barbara and I went to the stables. We got there a little after 7:00 a.m. We gave their horse named MOB BOSS—I didn't know the reason for the name—some feed and some carrots.

The horse is a beautiful animal. We then took it out to a pasture to run around, bucking, and feeling his oats. They have special black T-shirts made, with MB (in white) on the front and Mob Boss's mob on the back. This T-shirt was only given to a selected small group of people. We hung around there for a while.

Then one of the workers came by on a golf cart and told me to hop on. We went out to several of the pastures and brought the horses back to the stables one at a time. We took turns driving the cart while the other one held the horse. That was fun.

Barbara arranged for me to actually ride a trotter around the track a few times. The horse did most of the work. I went three times around the track at a decent speed. I had to keep the horse on the outside part of the track for some reason.

Barbara and I drove back to the house and waited for Larry. I had a bite to eat. He arrived at 11:30 a.m. and had a sandwich. We talked for a while then walked the dogs.

I headed back for Baltimore at 12:30 p.m. and arrived a little after 3:00 p.m. Checked the car back in and was driven back to the hotel. I made a few calls and went down to the lobby to write in my journal. I will go out shortly to see what there was to do.

There was a convention of pop culture comic book collectors for three days—a very large group of young people dressed up in all sorts of weird costumes, and I do mean weird! I walked around the convention center for a long time, taking some of their pictures. Some of the ladies were dressed very sexily and provocatively.

I went across the street to a restaurant with outside seating at about 7:30 p.m. I had a ringside seat. After a while, I ordered some wine and food. I took my time because of all the many sights to see. It was about 10:00 p.m. when the weather started turning bad, so I got back to the hotel just before it started to rain. I called it a night. Another long and active day.

Friday, July 27

I am going to the breakfast room. Getting caught up on my journal. I'm also going to the computer room to transfer the handwritten onto the typed version. I will try to do that as often as possible to avoid doing so much when I get home.

The ball game starts at 7:10 p.m. I will get there early as usual. I hope it doesn't rain. But because of an important phone call that took about three hours and didn't accomplish a thing, now it's almost time to go to the game. I took the light rail to the ballpark. I had a quick drink at the restaurant I was at the other day and continued on to the game.

My timing was perfect in getting into the gates. I went down to the field dressed in the usual. There was a ball that came right in front of me, so I picked it up. Then I moved to the other side of the field behind the first-base dugout where the Oakland A's were warming up. I did get five autographs: #16 Josh Reddick (outfielder), #28 Eric Sogard (infielder), #54 Travis Blackley (pitcher), #22 Chris Carter (infielder), #38 Andrew Carignan (pitcher), and Rick Dempsey, the MVP of the 1983 World Series who was now the postgame announcer for the Oakland A's.

After that, I walked around until the game started and found a seat thirty rows behind third base. The game was a good one. It went back and forth, each team taking the lead. The game was tied 9–9 in the ninth inning. The A's scored five runs, seven won the game 14–9.

While the game was going on, there were a number of people interested in my Astros jersey. One young man came over and sat down next to me with a lot of questions. It didn't bother me at all. He was drunk but not obnoxious. He even told me to stand up at one time. He even bought me a beer. I walked back to the restaurant across from the convention center and had a beer before walking back to the hotel. It was after midnight when I got back to the hotel.

Saturday, July 28

Woke up at 6:30 a.m., packed, and took the light rail to the airport. Got checked in and went to the gate. The plane boarded on time. Arrived in Atlanta at 12:30 p.m. Took the MARTA (Atlanta's transit system—a very good one) to the hotel.

My hotel was one block from the exit of the MARTA. Checked in and went to the liquor store and restocked. It was about 3:00 p.m. now, and I was good and hungry. There was a Mexican restaurant next door, so I had a good lunch and a margarita.

There were some people sitting across from me that were drinking a special margarita. It was served in a large round glass with a small Corona beer upside down in the glass. So when you drank the margarita, the beer would slowly empty into it. I will have to try this out in Houston.

Got caught up with my journal while I had lunch. I was very tired, so I went back to the hotel and rested for a while. I got up and went to the computer room and was able to transfer four pages from my journal into the computer and print them. Of course this took me a long time. Now it was close to midnight, and I was hungry again. So I walked to another place close by and had something to eat and drink. It's now 2:00 a.m. Went back to the hotel and went to sleep.

Sunday, July 29

Got up at 9:30 a.m., went down, and transferred some more of my journal into the computer and printed it. Today is the Atlanta Braves game at 1:30 p.m. against the Philadelphia Phillies. I got on the MARTA then took the Braves shuttle to the ballpark just when they opened the gates. There were two retired Braves ballplayers signing autographs—Ryan Klesko and Rob Belloir. It was a good thing I got those because I didn't get any others. I was able to find a seat in the shade. I left in the eighth inning. The score was 5–1 Atlanta. Got back to the hotel and rested a few hours then went back down and transferred some more of my journal into the computer and printed them. At about 11:00 p.m., I found a place to eat something and retired for the evening. My next game was in Washington, DC.

Monday, July 30

Arrived in DC at 12:30 p.m. Took the shuttle to the hotel. Got to my room and had the idea of getting a walking stick from DC. I thought this would be the only one I would get. I went outside, and directly across the street were two men trimming branches from trees. I explained to one of them what I was doing. So he helped me with his saw, and I instantly got a good stick.

I went back to the hotel and asked what the best way to get to the ballpark was and where there was a good restaurant. The subway was the answer to both. The subway was only a few blocks away and a very easy route. I took the subway to the area of the good restaurants. Sure enough, I saw a McCormick & Schmick's on a corner. I wasn't ready to eat yet, so I walked around some.

I passed by the Smithsonian American Art Museum with a large and colorful bronze statue of a cowboy on his horse in the front and on the top steps. I wanted my picture taken. I wanted my picture taken with that in the background. So I waited until someone came toward me and asked if they wouldn't mind taking my picture. The first person didn't speak enough English.

Then a young lady came walking up, so I asked her if she wouldn't mind, and she said yes. I noticed a slight accent. I asked her where she was from. She told me she was from Denmark. She looked like she was from that area, with long blond hair and blue eyes. After she took my picture, I continued walking and talking with her. She was here by herself. She was a student, and during the three summer months, she was traveling around the USA. Her last stop will be NYC for nine days and then go back to Denmark. She leaves tomorrow for NYC (Tuesday. the thirty-first). I asked her if she had eaten yet. She said no, so I asked her to join me for dinner at McCormick & Schmick's. She agreed.

It was now after 6:00 p.m., and we were both hungry. I ordered a glass of chardonnay. She enjoyed wine as much as I did. We talked a lot more and ordered dinner. We each had three glasses of white wine, and with the cheese course, we had a glass of red. She couldn't finish the cheese, so she took it with her. We had the waiter take some pictures of us before we left.

Both of us felt like going to a bar to have another drink. We found a bar and went in. She had a beer because she likes beer also. I had a double shot of tequila and sipped on it slowly. We talked some more, and she wrote down her name and address in Denmark. While we were having dinner, I couldn't resist calling my friend Moe in Houston. When I got him on the phone, I let her talk to him. I told her he calls me Frank. They had a great conversation.

After we finished our drinks, she said it was time for her to get back to where she was staying. I asked if she wanted to come back with me but she said no. So I left it at that. We went our separate ways, but what an unexpected pleasure the evening turned out to be. It was after 1:00 a.m. when I got back to my hotel.

Tuesday, July 31

It's about 10:30 a.m. I went down to the lobby and wrote in my journal. I did go on a bus tour around DC. One could get on and off the bus wherever and whenever, as often as you wanted. I saw most of the historical monuments, museums, and landmarks from the bus. It was about 1:00 p.m. when I started. I took a lot of pictures.

At the Potomac River, I got off and walked down around the harbor until I came to a place that served lunch with a bar right on the river. I was now starting to be on a little bit of a time schedule. After I got back on the bus, it started to rain ever so slightly. They handed out these lightweight, thin, clear ponchos. After a while, it stopped raining.

I wanted to make one more stop at the Lincoln Memorial and took some pictures. It was most impressive. Since I was already in my baseball attire, I just got off the bus and caught the train to the ballpark. It was 5:30 p.m. by then. I did manage to get #24 Ty Wiggigton to sign my jersey (an outfielder for the Phillies). The ballpark had a restaurant—two bars that also had two rows of seating on the outside that also had food and bar service. I put my name on the waiting list for a table outside.

In the meantime, I talked to a young couple from the Philadelphia area. They were both nineteen years old and a lot of fun to talk to. We shared a table outside. No one asked them for ID, so they were served beers. They already had a few beers before we were seated. I bought a round of beers. They ordered a chicken and fries basket. The game started at 7:10 p.m. and was over about 10:30 p.m. I took the train back to the hotel and turned in. Another full day.

Wednesday, August 1

Had a wake-up call for 7:00 a.m. I didn't bother with the shuttle but took the subway back to the airport. Cost $3.90. Arrived at the airport at 8:00 a.m. Went through security and luckily went to the gate because they had booked me on an earlier flight. Instead of 10:30, I left at 9:30 a.m. Arrived in Chicago at 10:45 a.m. Got my bags and took the shuttle to the Hyatt about twelve noon, got checked in, went to my room, and unpacked because I was staying for nine days. Then I went to a Chase bank branch and got some more cash. Went to a supermarket nearby, bought some necessary supplies, and went back to my room, which was a small suite at a very reduced rate thanks to Danielle (Mark's daughter) who works at the Hyatt.

It was now 3:00 p.m. So I enjoyed a snack from some of the things I bought. Now it's 4:00 p.m., so I mixed myself a large drink and went down to the lobby to write in my journal. My first game here was on Friday, August 3, 7:10 p.m. White Sox versus LA Angels.

I also left a voice mail for Donnie that I was here and everything was great. The plan was to get together one evening to have dinner with Chip and Donnie at a restaurant of their choice. I will try to book a fishing charter and go fishing on the lake one day. The hotel concierge gave me a list of fishing guides to call. I went back to my room and rested a while. I did make some calls but no luck. The problem was that I was by myself, and they didn't want to put me with another group of people.

Donnie returned my call. We will go out Thursday, August 2. After resting a bit, I went out to the Navy Pier, a large pier that went out quite a long way with a lot of rides, shops, and places to eat and drink. It had one of the largest Ferris wheels (if not the largest). There were also a good number of large and small boats for different cruises one could take that were lined up.

Tonight there was a fireworks display at 9:30 over the water. I found a good place to watch it from. It lasted a good twenty minutes. After I walked back to a restaurant named after Harry Caray's, the very famous long-time announcer for the Cubs. It was very nice. It was midnight when I got back to the hotel and went to bed.

Thursday, August 2

Went down to the business center and transferred some more of my journals into the computer and got caught up writing in my journal as well. You must understand it took me four hours to type two or three pages. It was 11:30 a.m. so I went up to my room and brought some of the leftovers back down and had lunch.

I decided to take a walk along Lake Shore Drive where an awful lot of powerboats and sailboats were anchored. I finally found what I called a secret passageway between buildings to get through to the street. I walked a long way, but there was really nothing of interest to see. I walked back, and there was only one place you could sit down and have a drink without being in a private club.

I sat down and had a glass of wine or two. There was a man sitting by himself and also having a glass of wine. We started talking. He also told me of an Italian restaurant I should try that was owned and operated by a relative of Al Capone. I told him what I was doing in Chicago and what I still was going to do. We talked for a good long time.

When I got back to the hotel, I was able to make reservations for two boat cruises. The first one on Friday, the third, at twelve noon. It goes around the river and into the lake. It takes ninety minutes. The other one was a dinner cruise on Saturday, the fourth, at 8:30 p.m. till 11:00 p.m.

Now it was time to meet up with Chip and Donnie at 7:30 p.m. They knew of a small and good neighborhood pizza place that they go to often. Chip did the ordering. We split a salad that was more than just a salad and was plenty for the three of us and a large pizza that we split. They have their own unique way of cooking the pizza with a special crust. We had some wine and must have talked for two hours. They were in the process of looking for a home. I told them a bit about some of my baseball experiences. I took a cab back to the hotel at 10:00 p.m. and went to bed.

Friday, August 3

Got up at 9:30 a.m., went to the grocery store for something, then went back to the hotel room and wrote in my journal till 11:30 then went to the docks to go on my first cruise at twelve noon. We went up the Chicago River. The guide pointed out all the historical buildings and landmarks. Then we went through a set of locks that led into Lake Michigan. I took a few pictures. The whole cruise was very interesting but too much info.

The day was perfectly clear and warm. It was a very worthwhile cruise. It's now 2:00 p.m. I got back to the hotel, brought my leftover pizza, and a beer down to the area on the first floor and sat down at a table, catching up on writing in my journal. It's about 2:30 p.m., and I'm getting some glimpses of the Summer Olympics on TV every now and then.

There was a very well-known music festival in town for the weekend called Lollapalooza, taking place at Grant Park. I was able to get a ticket for this Sunday.

I left the hotel for the White Sox game at 5:00 p.m. It was easy to get there by the L train—one train and one stop. Got to the ballpark at 5:30 with my usual outfit on. The game was between the Sox and LA Angels. I went down to the field. I positioned myself between three or four small kids. A ball was tossed in our direction, so I reached up and caught it. I didn't feel bad because a ball tossed to me by Lance Berkman was caught by a kid.

There was a second ball tossed that I caught and gave to one of the kids. Then I moved behind the third-base dugout and got autographs from #18 Andrew Romine, infielder for the Angels. Then I saw the White Sox bullpen and remembered the conversation I had with their bullpen catcher Mark Salas in KC. So I stood where he could see me, and he did; he remembered me also with my Astros jersey on. He couldn't believe I was there. He came over and talked to me again, BUT this time, he was laughing, and we had a totally friendly conversation, NOT like in KC.

I told him how many people I have told about our first conversation. He laughed when he heard that. While I was at the bullpen, I got an autograph from #65 Nate Jones, pitcher for the White Sox, and #43 Addison Reed, pitcher for the Angels. I walked around until the start of the game and sat down thirty rows behind third base.

Both teams scored early. It was 4–3 Angels until the seventh, when the Sox went ahead. The Angels tied it up in the eighth. In the tenth, the Sox got the first batter on base and the next batter hit a walk-off HR. This was one of the better games so far.

After the game, a lady broadcaster for ESPN was interviewing the player that hit the HR when she got a face full of pie. I got a good picture of it. I left shortly after that. It was after 11:00 p.m. by then. I took the train back to the hotel. All the restaurants in the area were closed. I went to my room and had some cheese wine that I had bought and came in handy. It was well after 1:00 a.m. when I went to sleep.

A side note: because the Astros will be in the American League next year, I plan on going to see the White Sox when they play here and maybe say hello to the bullpen catcher.

Saturday, August 4

Got up and moving after 10:00 a.m. and went to the Walgreens store and developed at least twelve pictures with some text on some of them. I went to the Subway store and got a foot-long sandwich and took it back to the hotel. I had half of it and a beer and sat down on the main floor of the hotel and ate. I also had time to delete some of the pictures and also wrote in my journal. I am also going to send some things through FedEx that I don't need back to Houston.

Donnie sent a very nice platter of hors d'oeuvres and cheese that I will enjoy some time later. I also was able to transfer some more of my journal into the computer. My dinner cruise is tonight at 8:30 p.m. But a savvier storm came up at 4:30 p.m. with high winds and rain, so I called the cruise line and was able to reschedule my dinner cruise for Wednesday night, August 8. Luckily, my VIP concert tickets are for Sunday, the fifth. I went back up to my room and enjoyed some of the platter Donnie sent me. I stayed in my room and watched TV the rest of the evening. But I accomplished a lot during the day.

Sunday, August 5

Went back to Walgreens and developed some more pictures. Some of them were of Larry and Barbara at their home in Ocean View, Delaware. I made some duplicates to send to them later. It's noon, so I took the other half of my sandwich and a beer down to the lobby and had lunch before going to the music festival.

I walked there and arrived about 2:30 p.m. There were a good number of people gathering with a lot more coming in later. There were two main stages for the different bands plus other smaller stages in other locations in the area that bands would perform. Since I bought a VIP ticket, that enabled me to sit under a tent between the two stages with folding chairs and some sofa-type seating. Because of the VIP area, I could eat and drink as much as I wanted to at no charge.

There happened to be a small SUV sponsored by Tito's Vodka made in Texas represented in the area. The SUV was modified with couches, a TV, and a bar—very cool. The VIP tent was positioned between the two stages but about two hundred yards from them. At first I was disappointed, but as it turned out, it was the best deal. There were several food stations and bars set up just outside of the tent area that were all free.

I did sit in the Tito's SUV for a while and enjoyed the hospitality. I went back to the tent and sat down next to two couples. They were very familiar with the program because they have been here several years in a row. Two of them were from Canada. The other two were locals. They sort of adopted me. They knew of a very well-known band from Canada that was playing at another small stage nearby. So we all walked over there to listen. I didn't know what to expect when I got there, so I brought a flask of margaritas just in case, and it came in handy. We watched the band from Canada, and I passed around the margaritas. I have some pictures of a few people, and they took some pictures of me with them.

After we got back to the tent, the four people went their own way. It was after 5:00 p.m. now, and I was getting hungry, so I helped myself to the buffet and had a good dinner. It was finally getting dark. The crowd was actually getting larger. I stayed there until at least 9:30 p.m. and walked back to the hotel. I bought Chip and Donnie each a Lollapalooza cap and had a picture of us developed and left it with the receptionist at Donnie's office to give the next day when she got back. I walked back to the hotel and went to bed.

Monday, August 6

I came down to the lobby at 9:30 a.m. and wrote in my journal. Then went to FedEx to use their computer to transfer some more to the computer. It took about three hours. Donnie gave me some names of some restaurants to go to. Still no luck on the fishing charter. I went to lunch at 12:30 p.m.

Went to a place Donnie recommended for lunch by the name of the Purple Pig just up the street on Michigan Avenue—a very busy, upscale, casual place. They had a lot of unusual items on the menu. They were out of the two things I ordered, so I selected something simple. It took a very long time to be served. By the time I left there, it was 3:00 p.m.

I was told where there were some beaches along Lake Michigan. I walked for a very long way. I passed a model who was having her picture taken in a small bikini. So I took some pictures also. Why not! It was a beautiful day.

I got my feet wet in the lake. It was a little bit cold, but not unbearable. There were a large number of volleyball nets set up on the beach with an equal number of people playing. I ended up at the far end of the beach where there was a restaurant and bar available only on the second floor. It was outside overlooking the beach. It was a shame it took so long to be fed because I wasn't very hungry yet. I did order a guacamole salad, some chips, and a frozen margarita. I ate a little of the guacamole and took the rest with me.

The sun was starting to set, so I started back. It was a good long walk, and I enjoyed it. I took a few more pictures on the way back. Got back to the hotel just after dark and called it a night.

Tuesday, August 7

Woke up at 6:00 a.m. and watched some TV. Got up and dressed and went to the lobby at 11:00 a.m. I brought my camera and journal down with me. I was able to delete the pictures that were no good and wrote in my journal. I went back upstairs and brought back down the leftovers from yesterday. I went out and bought a road atlas of the USA. I drew lines from city to city in the order of when I was in that city and numbered them. It came out better than I expected. I also got a well-needed haircut.

I didn't do much else until 5:45 p.m. when I started out by bus to the improv comedy show I went to see. The bus cost $2.25. I came back by cab, $12. I got to the theater at 6:30 p.m. The doors opened at 7:00 p.m. I was the first in line and was taken to a very good seat up front. A waitress came by and took drink orders. I ordered a double vodka tonic so I wouldn't have to order another one later.

This was a different format from the other comedy clubs I've seen. There were six comedians, three men and three women—ALL very different and VERY talented. This was entirely different from the regular comedy shops where each comedian does their own stand-up routine. The six of them did an enormous amount of short and clever skits, sometimes using just two people, other times using more people. That covered a large amount of topics.

Just before the first intermission, they asked for a volunteer from the audience to be part of the skit. He happened to be very clever and fit into the skit almost like he was part of the act but he wasn't. He really was good. The comedians were exceptionally versatile. The thing I enjoyed the most was that it was live. When a mistake was made, and there were, it was interesting to watch how well they were able to ad-lib and cover up their mistakes.

There was a third act that was mostly improv. They had the audience taking more part in it. It was amazing what they came up with. This was the part I liked the best. But the whole show was great and lasted for three hours. The name of the theater was the Second City, a very well-known and respected comedy theater. I left there after 11:00 p.m. I walked to where there were a string of restaurants and got to one just before the kitchen closed. I was good and hungry. I ordered a cup of soup and a main course and a glass of wine. I left there after 1:00 p.m. and took a cab to the hotel. I knew I couldn't find my way back by bus (that's why the cab).

Wednesday, August 8

I woke up at 6:00 a.m. and watched TV until 9:30 a.m. I looked over some of my airline and baseball tickets. Everything was still in order. I reconfirmed my shuttle service to the airport. I also called Joannie Wecksler in NYC and reconfirmed some dates and times with her. I'm now about three-fourths of the way through my trip.

It's about 11:30 a.m., and I'm down in the lobby with my journal, some cheese, bread, and red wine. The only thing I have planned for the day was the dinner cruise at 8:30 p.m. that I rescheduled for today. I also had some more pictures developed. When I was in the lobby, I noticed that this was the least busy I've seen the hotel.

I left the hotel about 3:30 p.m. and walked along the beach. It started to rain ever so slightly. Hardly enough to get the streets wet. I turned around and headed back toward the Navy Pier where the ship for the dinner cruise was anchored. There are a lot of shops that were indoors, so I walked around there for a couple of hours and bought a few small souvenirs. Then I stopped at one of the bars and had a glass of wine.

We could board the ship at 6:00 p.m. I called it a ship because it's the size of a small cruise ship without the staterooms. There were two levels for dining and three levels for observation decks. They gave me a table next to the window that I had requested. There were tables of twos, fours, and sixes throughout the dining room. There was a server assigned to a section. All the servers were very accommodating. The package I bought included dinner and two drinks. Because I switched my reservation from Sunday to Wednesday, I was given an extra $60 credit to be used for drinks, wine, or gratuity. I felt like having a dirty martini before ordering. The menu was very simple and limited but very good. It did stop raining just as we got under way.

We had two hours to eat before the fireworks started, so there was no rush. It was a three-course dinner—soup or appetizer, MC, and dessert. After dinner, we went up to one of the observation decks to watch the fireworks. I went to the top one where you could smoke. I did bring a cigar just in case. So I lit up. The fireworks started at 9:30 p.m. The evening turned out to be beautiful. The fireworks lasted about twenty or thirty minutes. We docked shortly after that. I got back to the hotel at 10:30 p.m.

Thursday, August 9

Woke up at 6:00 a.m. but stayed in bed till 9:30 a.m. Got up, took a shower, and did some packing. Went down to the lobby to write in my journal. Also I wanted to find a T-Mobile store because the back of my phone didn't stay on. I also wanted to find the Italian restaurant that a man recommended to me when I first got here.

I'll go to the Cubs game tonight f the weather permits. There is a slight chance of rain. I got directions to go to the restaurant by bus. It was very easy and cost only $4.50 round-trip. The restaurant was very decorated simply—simple tables and chairs with no tablecloths. they had a lot of very old photographs of some very famous Italian celebrities on the walls.

The owner a long time was a cousin of Al Capone. It might be my imagination, but some of the customers dressed and sounded like Mafia. I had a cup of minestrone soup, the house salad, and the veal marsala. The wine was served in a clear, hard plastic cup, not a wine glass. It was well worth the experience.

Took the bus back to the hotel and changed into my Astros outfit. I took the L train—$5 round-trip. When I got to the ballpark, it started to rain very lightly. I bought one of those flimsy, clear plastic ponchos. I went into one of the many bars surrounding the ballpark and had a drink. The game was now on a rain delay. Because of the rain, there was no batting practice and no chance for autographs.

The delay lasted one and a half hours. The Reds and the Cubs scored early. The game was tied three all in the seventh. Then it started to rain again but not enough to postpone the game. It continued to rain off and on. I was afraid it would go into extra innings, but the Cubs in the bottom of the eighth with a man on base hit a HR. The game ended 5–3 Cubs. The announcer cried out, "The Cubs win! The Cubs win!"

I took the L back to Lake Street where I got on. It was raining harder now. I was glad I kept the poncho. When got back to the hotel, I had a good snack compliments from Donnie. Went to sleep at 1:30 a.m. Left a wake-up call for 6:00 a.m.

Friday, August 10

Got up, finished packing, and caught the shuttle for the airport. Next stop, NYC. Got to the airport in plenty of time. Went to a bar just across from my gate and had a Baileys and coffee and wrote in my journal. The Mets game was scheduled for tonight. I just now found out that all flights to NYC were canceled because of bad weather in NYC. So I booked a flight from Chicago to

Boston that leaves at 8:45 p.m. and arrives in Boston at midnight on the eleventh.

Saturday, August 11

When I arrived in Boston, I took the free shuttle to the Amtrak train station. The train from Boston to NYC left at 6:45 a.m. I had a long sleepless five hours at the station. I was in business class, which was a little bit nicer than coach. It took about five hours to get to NYC. I slept along the way.

The train trip was amazing. When we passed some trees on both sides of the train, it looked like something out of *Star Trek* because we were traveling at speeds of 125 miles per hour (warp speed, Scotty). We did pass through Rhode Island and Connecticut. There were some quaint small fishing towns we went through. I had my camera with me but didn't think of taking pictures, but I managed to take a few.

I arrived at Pennsylvania Station at 10:30 a.m. and walked to the hotel. Needless to say, I missed the Mets game. But out of thirty-one games, that was the only one I missed. Pretty good record. The rest of the planned events were back on schedule.

The hotel was small but nice. I did a load of wash that took one hour. I had some peanuts from a Southwest Airlines flight that I snacked on. I didn't want to spoil my appetite because I was going to have dinner with my friend that I've known for so long, Aja Zanova, a world champion figure skater. She was born in the Czech Republic. She has won several gold medals. We have the same birth date.

I rested some more before going out. I got ready at 5:30 p.m. and had to wear a suit and tie. It was the only time I wore them. I took a cab to her apartment on Fifth Avenue. I had been there once before four years ago. She took me to the restaurant, 21 Club. She treated me that time. It was my treat this time.

I arrived at her apartment at 6:00 p.m. Our reservation was for 7:30 p.m., so we had plenty of time to talk. She opened a bottle of champagne and talked about what we have been doing and finished the bottle. We took a cab to the Four Seasons restaurant, the most elegant and prestigious restaurant in NYC. Nothing to do with the Four Seasons hotel chain. Of course she knew the manager and the wait staff knew her. We were seated at the best table. I ordered a very fine bottle of French white Burgundy. We were given an appetizer, compliments of the house. I also ordered an appetizer. We finished the first wine then I ordered a bottle of red Bordeaux with our MC. I had the duck, and she ordered the rack of lamb. We split a chocolate Grand Marnier soufflé. We finished dinner about 11:00 p.m. We took a cab and dropped her off at her place and then I was taken to my hotel. That was it for Saturday. What a day!

Sunday, August 12

It's going to be a full day with cousin Joannie. I'm right outside my hotel door sitting on a bench, writing in my journal. It's another beautiful day in Gotham City. I'm going to have some more photos developed. Joannie and I will meet at 2:30 p.m. and go to a Broadway show. Then take a cruise around Manhattan island and then have dinner. My journal files are getting larger while my baseball tickets and airline ticket files are getting smaller and my miscellaneous files are growing.

I had a small bite to eat before meeting Joannie. We met in front of the theater. The play was *Porgy and Bess* by George Gershwin. Joannie bought tickets three rows from the stage, just to the left of center. The actors, the singing, the dancing were all incredible. A very dramatic play. Immediately after the play was over, we hopped into a cab and went directly to the Hudson River docks to get on the cruise.

The play was over at 6:00 p.m., and we boarded the boat at 6:30 p.m. We found some seats on the outside deck. The weather was ideal. I bought myself a good drink. Sitting beside us was a couple from Houston. While I was gone, Joannie told them all about me, and they knew about Maxim's. The cruise started in daylight and ended when it was dark. We passed by the Statue of Liberty and a lot of other famous landmarks. After dark, we saw the whole city light up. That was something. It was after 9:00 p.m. We took a cab back to where Joannie would catch her bus and found a place to have dinner. She caught her bus, and I walked around Times Square and then walked back to the hotel probably after 1:00 a.m.

Monday, August 13

Got up, took a shower, and sat outside to write in my journal. I went back to Aja's apartment and gave her some of the pictures I had developed of the two of us and had her sign the back of my jersey.

Joannie and I are going to the NY Yankees game tonight at 7:10 p.m. She loves the Yankees. I went back to my hotel and rested for a while. Before I got back to the hotel, I stopped at a camera store and bought another memory chip for my camera. Before leaving the hotel, I had a few leftovers just to tide me over. I took the subway to the stadium. Very easy. I got there early and called Joannie to let her know which gate I was at. Because the game was a sellout, we went directly to our seats.

The Texas Rangers took the early lead. The Yanks hit a grand-slam HR in the fourth inning. We left the game in the sixth inning. The final score was 8–2 Yankees. We stopped at a restaurant and had a bite to eat. Then we went our own ways. The game must have just ended because when I got on the subway, it was packed.

Walked back to the hotel, did some packing, and left a wake-up call for 7:00 a.m.

Tuesday, August 14

The shuttle picked me up at 7:40 a.m. I got to the airport and checked in with plenty of time. Arrived in Detroit at 3:30 p.m. The only transportation to the hotel was by cab or limo. I took the limo this time because it was a fixed rate of $55. Got to the hotel at 4:30 p.m. Got settled and went back out to buy a few things and then walked around a bit. The Detroit River is just a few blocks from the hotel. I bought a Styrofoam cooler to put some things into and filled it with ice. The cooler has become very handy. I had some leftovers that I brought with me from NYC that needed to be kept cold. I enjoyed some of the leftovers this evening. It was too late to do anything else today, so I stayed in.

Wednesday, August 15

A totally different day from Tuesday. Got started at 11:30 a.m. Got on the bus right next to the hotel that took me to the bus station and took another bus into Canada, the town of Windsor in the province of Ontario. Bought some souvenirs. Found out where the best street with the best restaurant and bar was. I also bought some Cuban cigars.

My first stop was an Irish pub with outside seating. I ordered a beer that came in a special boot-shaped glass. That was a MUST have. After that, I walked around close to the river.

There was a BBQ ribs festival starting the next day and lasting through the weekend. But this was absolutely nothing at all like our BBQ cook-off. They only had six contestants competing. I continued walking around and went to another bar that also had outside seating, so I had a glass of wine and a cigar. It's now 3:30 p.m. I sat there for about two hours. I talked to some of the people there. There was also an attractive young lady sitting by herself. She must have been a regular because she was known there. I watched her take a very real-looking mustache out of her purse and put it on under her nose. I couldn't resist having my picture taken with her.

She was joined by a girlfriend and left shortly after. I asked where there was a good but not fancy restaurant. They pointed to one just a few blocks away. So after a short time, I walked over there. It was close to 8:30 p.m. now. I had a good dinner and started back to the bus terminal. I caught all three buses that eventually took me to the hotel. It was after midnight when I got back.

Thursday, August 16

Another great day. It's 11:00 a.m., and I'm writing in my journal. I will ship some more things back to Houston that I don't need to carry around with me. I went to the UPS store and shipped nine and a half pounds back to Houston. I also found a pair of sweatpants to replace the ones I had.

I caught two buses that took me back to Canada. I made it just in time to board a cruise boat that toured the Detroit River. The tour wasn't anything special, but there were two young ladies on board that I was able to sit next to. The older one was twenty-two and her sister was fourteen. We talked practically the whole time.

When we landed, we went to the Ribfest. We were all good and hungry at this time. There were six stations that offered ribs, chicken, and more. There was a separate area for beer. You could go in and out of the beer area and buy ribs as often as you wanted. You had to buy tickets for the beer. We were able to hit four of the cook stations. I have pictures of us on the boat and at the Ribfest.

After we were stuffed, we walked around and looked at the other booths that were there. Sadly the twenty-two-year-old and her sister were picked up by her boyfriend. But I did get a big hug from both of them. It was about 8:30 p.m., so I went back to the pub I had been before. I lit up a cigar and had a drink. I walked back to the bus terminal and caught the two buses back to the hotel. It was after midnight when I got to sleep.

Friday, August 17

Got up and out at 11:00 a.m. after writing in my journal. Went back to Canada and to the Ribfest. I was able to go to the two booths I had missed before and got a souvenir tin cup that I wanted and I made it back in time to go to the ball game. Before going back, I wanted a stick from Canada to add to my collection. I found the perfect stick and headed back. I was able to bring the stick back through customs.

I made it back just in time to change and take the hotel's complimentary shuttle to the game. Got there at 5:00 p.m. and walked in to the stadium. The place I was at didn't seem to be very good, so I moved to another location that turned out to be much better. I got autographs #10 Adam Jones, a pitcher for Baltimore, and #11 Robert Andino, infielder for Baltimore. Both teams scored often until the eighth inning when Prince Fielder hit a two-run HR, his second of the game.

This ballpark had some unique seats that looked more like very nice wooden chairs with arms and a cushion and a table between chairs. I sat there until someone came, and I had to move. Since there was a large crowd, I went to my assigned seat. I left the game early and walked to an area called Greektown. There were restaurants and bars all around and a casino called Greektown. I went to a Cajun restaurant that served seafood and steaks. They also had a two-piece band. I was too late to get the shuttle back, but I wouldn't have found it anyway. I took a cab back to the hotel. Wasn't far.

Saturday, August 18

Got a wake-up call at 5:00 a.m. Got about four hours' sleep. Got to the airport in plenty of time. Arrived in Boston, Massachusetts, at 3:30 p.m. Got some sleep on the plane. I found out about the subway that took me closer to the hotel. With a little help, I was able to carry two bags and my stick from Canada to the hotel.

First thing I did was to ship the stick along with a few other things back to Houston. After settling, I had a good plate of leftovers and a beer in the lobby. The temperature in Beantown was in the sixties and overcast. No more shorts and short-sleeved shirts for a while.

It's now 6:00 p.m., and I'm caught up in my journal. My game here is only on Tuesday, August 21. I leave on the twenty-second. I will have plenty of time for sightseeing. I was given the names of some very good and popular oyster and seafood places. I had nothing to do for a few hours. I wasn't hungry yet, so I did a load of wash. Now it was 9:00 p.m., so I took a cab to the oyster house, which was recommended to me. There was a line outside the door waiting to get in. I saw another oyster house just down the street, so I went there. I was seated right away. I had a very good dinner and took my time eating. Caught a cab back to the hotel.

Sunday, August 19

Got up at 9:00 a.m. and wrote in my journal. Decided to go to the Naval Yard and look around. The USS *Constitution* (Old Ironsides) was docked there and also a WWII battleship. Old Ironsides was out for a sail around the harbor. I looked at the battleship for a while and took some pictures. There were eight men dressed like British soldiers with muskets. Went to the *Constitution* museum and bought a hat and a pin. When I got to the harbor, it was 11:00 a.m. At about 12:30, I decided to take a bus tour around Boston. You could get on and off the bus at different stops. I got off at a place called Chelsea Market, a huge area with shops and restaurants just for pedestrians. I had lunch at a very nice restaurant with outside seating.

There were many individuals and groups performing unique acts. I took some pictures. I got back on the bus. The tour was interesting, but a lot of the historical sites were no longer there. We got back to the harbor at 5:00 p.m. The USS *Constitution* was back. I went aboard, but it was almost time to close. So I will come back tomorrow. On the way back, I saw an old-fashioned Italian funeral parade with a small band and a small statue of a saint that was very ornamentally decorated and was very heavy. It was carried by five people on each side of their shoulders. There were ribbons streaming down with money attached to the ribbons. They made stops at almost all the bars along the way. More pictures. There was a CVS on the way back to the hotel, so I had some pictures developed. It was 9:00 p.m. when I finished. I stopped to eat at a sports bar nearby the hotel to have dinner. It was very good. Then I walked back to the hotel.

Monday, August 20

I am going to a small fishing town in Maine. It's 10:30 a.m. now. I looked at a train schedule and a train was leaving for Portland, Maine, at 11:05 a.m. I took a cab to the train station and made it just in time. Arrived in Portland at 1:30 p.m. I went to an area of town called Old Port, a very nice area with shops, restaurants, and a number of different boat tours, including a whale-watching tour. But I was too late for that. There was a lobster-catching boat tour. So I signed up for the 5:00 p.m. trip. They stopped at their own lobster traps. We all took turns bringing in the traps. They measure each lobster to see if they are big enough to keep. We all were given thick rubber gloves and aprons to wear.

It was a clear, cool beautiful day. Took some pictures. The trip lasted one hour. When I got off the boat, I heard some live music coming from the bar just on the other dock across from us. So I went over there. The group was a bluegrass country band. There was a good crowd.

As I walked through the place looking for a seat, a young man asked me about my sunglasses. They had bright-orange rims that I got for free from Tito's Vodka, so I gave them to him. He and his two friends thought that was a neat thing to do. So they invited me to sit down with them. So I did. They were just out of college. They shared their pitcher of beer with me, and I bought the next pitcher. I told them what I was doing, and we shared some very funny experiences. There was a table next to us with four lovely ladies that we engaged in our conversation. Guess who was the instigator? You're right. We had some pictures taken with them. I wanted to stay longer, but the train back to Boston left at 7:55 p.m., and I didn't want to miss it. Although it was tempting.

When I got back, I got a call from the people in Knoxville, Tennessee. They recommended a hotel for me to stay at that would be convenient for all of us. I made the reservations for the change in flights and the hotel reservations when I got back to my hotel. It took some time doing it and was very late when I finally got through to what I wanted to do.

Tuesday, August 21

The game tonight will be Boston versus LA Angels at 7:10 p.m. I took my time getting ready. By now, I knew my way around by subway. Since I only had a very short time on the USS *Constitution* on Sunday, and they were closed Monday, this was a very good time to go and get back in with plenty of time for the game. I got there at 12:30 p.m. I remembered the street with the Italian bars and restaurants, so I stopped in for lunch at one of them.

The waitress was as Italian as anyone could be. You sat where she told you to. No questions asked. I ordered some veal and a glass of pinot gris. Both were very good. I couldn't finish it all, so I took it to go. Then I went on a self-guided tour of the ship, and I did manage to get away with a belaying pin to add to my collection. Took the two subways back to the hotel, changed, and went to the game at 4:30 p.m.

This time they only opened the gate a short time before BP was over. I didn't get any ballplayer's autographs but did get one of the Boston TV personalities to sign and also his very attractive assistant to sign. Once more, because there was a very large crowd, I went to my assigned seat. There was a home run hit clear over the Green Monster wall and clear out of the ballpark. That doesn't happen very often. The Angels won 5–3. It was close to 11:00 p.m. I walked back to the hotel and had a midnight snack. Left a wake-up call for 4:30 a.m. and finished packing before going to bed.

Wednesday, August 22

I took two subways to the airport with my two bags and made it to the airport in plenty of time. The plane made one stop in New Jersey. Arrived in Philadelphia, Pennsylvania, at 3:30 p.m. There was a free shuttle that dropped me off just across the street from my hotel. After putting my things away, I went to the lobby to inquire about some sightseeing, etc. Made a few calls, got some directions, and went to a bar and grill connected to the hotel for a bite to eat at 5:30 p.m. and caught up with my journal. It's hard to catch up after not writing in my journal for two days and remembering everything.

I was given the name of a place famous for their Philly cheesesteak sandwiches. The next game was on Friday, August 24 at 7:05 p.m. I took a walk to the ballpark. There weren't any bars or restaurants around the park except one very large and noisy game room, disco, and bar. That wasn't what I had in mind. There were a lot of historical sites to see before the next game. There was also a game tonight, so there would be a lot of people around.

It's now 9:00 p.m. I found out that Philly was divided into many different parts. I took a cab to the place that was recommended to me for the famous sandwich. It was a restaurant that didn't serve any alcoholic beverages, so I took my sandwich back to the hotel, went to my room, and brought it down with a beer and sat in their lounge to eat. The sandwich was OK but nothing special. After I was finished, I went to bed.

Thursday, August 23

I went out at 10:30 a.m. and took a bus tour of the city that you could get on and off anytime. Saw a lot of historic sites and took a lot of pictures. I got off three times. The first time was Pennsylvania Academy of the Fine Arts where Rocky climbed the seventy-two steps. I didn't even try. But I had a picture taken of me at the top of the steps, smoking a cigar. I hope to put a good caption on that picture.

Got back on the bus. As we passed, we were passing a bar named Dirty Frank's. The bus driver pointed out to us that on the two sides at the front of the bar were a large painted mural with a lot of famous people and things with the name Frank somehow connected to it. I got off at the next closest stop and walked back to the bar. This was my second stopping-off place. I took some pictures of the two sides. Then I had to go inside and had a drink just out of curiosity. It was a little after 1:00 p.m. There were only two people and the lady bartender in the bar at this time. When I asked for the check and wanted to pay by credit card, she showed me a black T-shirt with white letters on the back—Cash Only—and also in white letters on the front—Dirty Frank's.

Since my friend nicknamed me Frank, I had to buy this T-shirt. But I insisted that the bartender sign it using blue and yellow colors, the colors of the Pennsylvania flag. I was able to find some acrylic colors for her to use. She took a long time painting her name just like her very own signature and the date and Philadelphia in blue and yellow. It took her a good two hours, but it was well worth it.

It was about 4:00 p.m. and the bar started to get busy. The bartender knew almost all the people by name. I took some pictures of her showing the T-shirt. Also several times of me wearing the T-shirt at different times. I planned to send her some of the pictures. I left the bar at 5:00 p.m.

My third stop was the Liberty Bell. I had to take some pictures of that. I didn't get back on the bus because it was getting late. So I took a cab to another well-known Philly cheesesteak place. Again no alcohol was served and again it was disappointing. I took the sandwich back to the hotel. As I was walking back, I saw some loose bricks in the street, so I picked one up and brought it back with me.

Friday, August 24

I got up at 7:00 a.m. I painted on the brick, in yellow and blue, "Philadelphia Pa. 08-23-12." I'm catching up with my journal now. I took the brick and a few other things to be mailed back to Houston. Total weight: nine and a half pounds. Then I took three subways and a bus to New Jersey at a cost of $8 round-trip. I took a self-guided tour of the USS *New Jersey* battleship. A guided tour would have been too much info that you won't remember. There were some restricted areas that were blocked off with these red velvet ropes with brass knobs on top. So I unsecured one of them for another souvenir. I continued walking around for a long time. There was a lot of very interesting things to see. Took a lot of pictures.

On the way out, there was a small tiki-style bar. A beer sure was good about now. It was getting a little late, so I made my way back to Philly the same way I got to New Jersey—three subways and a bus. Had a quick bite to eat and changed into my uniform. The ballpark was also near where the Eagles played. Also the 76ers and ice hockey arena area. It was 5:30 p.m., and they were just opening the gates. I was wearing my Dirty Frank's T-shirt under my Astros jersey.

I went directly down to the field. I was able to get three autographs: # 47 Gio Gonzalez (pitcher), #25 Adam LaRoche (infielder), and #89 Joe Martinez (batting practice pitcher). All from the Washington Nationals. I then made my way past the third-base line. After BP and just before the game started, they let a few people into the playing field to help put the white chalk lines down. I got to help do that. Pretty cool.

I went back and stood at a long stainless steel counter where you could put what you were eating or drinking down on and watch the game. There were two very loud, obnoxious, and drunk guys right next to me. The fans seated right in front of them reported them to security. They had to be physically escorted out of the ballpark. The game was uneventful compared to that. Phillies won 4–2. I walked back to the hotel. There was a restaurant right next to the hotel. I had a very good dinner there. Took a doggie bag back to the hotel with me. Did some packing. It was 1:00 a.m. by now.

Saturday, August 25

Got up at 7:30 a.m., took a shower, got dressed, and checked out. I decided to take a cab instead of the bus to the Amtrak station. I'm in the café having some coffee and writing in my journal. I tried to contact the people in Knoxville to let them know about my plans and where I was staying, etc. There was no answer, so I left a voice mail. I will try again later.

Boarded the train to Pittsburgh, Pennsylvania. One of the cool things about going by train was you always can get to tour luggage. It comes in handy sometimes. I had some leftovers and a beverage that I made good use of. I get into Pittsburgh, Pennsylvania, at 8:00 a.m. I saw a lot of interesting sites along the way. There were a lot of Amish people in Pennsylvania. I saw one pulling by five or six horses plowing his field. The train followed some rivers for most of the trip. I also dozed off once in a while and played a lot of cards.

There was no mass transportation in Pittsburgh. So I shared a cab with a young lady. I went from the train station to my hotel that was near the airport. At first I was not too happy with the location, but it turned out to be the right choice. There was a bus that takes you from the airport into town and back for $3.75. I did forget to mention that at the game in Philly, there were five of the Summer Olympics gold medal winners. After I got checked in, I went down to the bar just in time to have dinner and a drink. After that I went to bed.

Sunday, August 26

The morning didn't look very promising weather-wise, but it cleared up. I got on the bus for downtown. One more thing I forgot to mention was that I saw a mouse in the subway and took a picture of it. I walked to the ballpark that was on the river. There were a lot of large and small boats cruising up and down the river and some of them were tied up together with people in it partying. I don't think they were interested in the game. I hope I got some good pictures.

There was a game that day. Pittsburgh was playing Milwaukee today. The score in the fifth inning was 6–0 Milwaukee. I walked into a bar that was right next to the stadium. They had the game on all the TV sets. I asked the bartender if he could put one of them on the Little League World Series and he did. It was Tennessee against Japan. Japan won 12–2 and Milwaukee won 7–0.

I asked the guy I was sitting next to if he knew of some other bars and restaurants nearby. He gave me a few names. The first place was Grille 36 owned by Jerome Bettis. The Hall of Fame player from the Pittsburgh Steelers. I sat down with a couple from Cleveland, Ohio. I had a glass of wine. We talked for a while. Then I walked down the street where the Steelers have their stadium and took some pictures. Then I went to the second place—an Irish pub that was like an Irish version of Hooters. I took my time at all the places. I went to the third place—a very good steak house. I took what I couldn't finish back with me to the hotel.

Monday, August 27

Got up at 10:30 a.m. and wrote in my journal. At 11:30 a.m., I stopped and had some of the leftovers and a beer. Since I got such a late start, I got dressed in my Astros attire. It's now about 1:00 p.m. I took the bus into town and went back to Jerome Bettis's place at about 2:00 p.m. I've been fighting a bit of a sinus cold but nothing serious. The weather was slowly getting a little worse and starting to look like it was going to rain.

At about 5:00 p.m., it started to drizzle a bit. I walked back to the Irish pub and sat next to two guys that were going to the game also. Of course we started talking and the subject of my trip came up. Because it was raining, there wasn't any BP. So I stayed at the bar. We could see on the TV when they would start the game. It stopped raining at 6:30 p.m.

The game was only delayed about thirty minutes from its original start time. One of the guys gave me his tickets, and I gave him mine. Their tickets were only three rows behind the third-base dugout where the Pirates were. WOW! The guy that had my tickets came and sat down very close to us. The guy I was with introduced me to a very well-known local TV announcer and called him over in the middle of his broadcast and told him what I was doing. But nothing came of it. I did get him to sign my jersey.

My guy got the attention of one of the starting pitchers, #27 Jeff Karstens, to come over between innings to sign my jersey also. ALL this that happened was so highly unlikely to happen it would be hard to believe but it did. It continued to rain on and off during the game but not enough to stop the game. St. Louis won 4–3 over Pittsburgh. It was too late to catch the bus back, so I took a cab at $40.

Tuesday, August 28

I flew out of Pittsburgh at 11:00 a.m. I was glad I was right near the airport. It took one hour to get to Toronto, Canada. I took a shuttle to the hotel and will take it back to the airport when I leave. I passed through customs OK. The hotel was only a few blocks from the ballpark and a few blocks from the CN tower. Very much like the Space Needle in Seattle, Washington, but over twice as high. It was after 4:00 p.m. when I got to the tower. I made dinner reservations to eat in their revolving restaurant for 5:30 p.m. That was the earliest you could make them. I walked around and bought some souvenirs.

Then it was time to go up to the restaurant. I was given a very nice table right next to the window. I had a very good three-course dinner with wine. I took the leftovers with me. It was 8:00 p.m., so I took my laundry and some change to the Sheraton Hotel because my hotel didn't have a Laundromat. I had to tell them I was staying here to be able to do my washing. During the wash cycle, I walked over to a very nice bar with outside seating. I sat down under a heat lamp. YES, a heat lamp. And it felt very good. After I finished my drink, I went back and put my stuff into the drying cycle and went back to the bar, ordered a drink, and lit up a cigar. Got up and gathered my laundry and went back to the hotel.

Wednesday, August 29

Getting caught up with my journal. Went to a pharmacy and bought some cold and allergy meds. It's now twelve noon. Got the leftovers and a large cup of wine and went to the hotel lobby and had lunch. It's 2:00 p.m. now. I got directions to go to what was known as the Waterfront, where they have boat tours. I got on what was called the Tall Ship Cruise. These were all sailing ships with three tall masts. It was a one and a half sail but nothing special. I was sitting next to a rope that wasn't properly secured. As it flapped around, it knocked my USS *New Jersey* cap off. I will be able to order another one when I get back to Houston.

After that tour, I got on another boat tour that took us across to an island just on the other side. It was a beautiful blue-sky day and just a bit cool. The boat wound its way through some small channels. The boat docked, and we were able to get off and be picked up again later. There was a lot to do and see. Many people brought picnics with them. I made my way to the beach. I took my socks off and rolled up my pants and walked in the water of Lake Ontario. The water was cool but not cold. I stopped for a quick beer before getting back on the boat. I went back to the hotel and rested for a couple of hours. I went back out at 10:00 p.m. I found a nice restaurant and bar. Had a late-night dinner and some wine. The soup I had was especially good. I might go back there for lunch.

Thursday, August 30

I got up at 9:00 a.m. Went down to the coffee shop and asked for a few packages of salt for gargling. I also took some of the DayQuil tablets. I'm now in the lobby writing in my journal. My cough and runny nose are still with me but not bad. The game is at 7:05 tonight. I didn't feel like doing very much, so I went back to my room and rested before going to the game. I got to the game just as they were opening the gates. Did get autographs from #56

Fernando Rodney, a relief pitcher, and #53 Alex Cobb, a starting pitcher for the Tampa Bay Rays. I tried going to a restaurant right next door to the hotel the night before, but it was closed. So I left the game at 8:45. I wanted to make sure this time I was going to be able to eat there. The baseball score ended 2–0 Blue Jays. I did have my picture taken with the Blue Jays mascot. The restaurant was very good. I'm glad I went back. I left a wake-up call for 5:00 a.m., but they didn't call me. Luckily, I woke up just after 5:00 a.m.

Friday, August 31

Got going at 5:00 a.m. Took the shuttle back to the airport. Went through all the checkpoints including customs. There were two gate changes for my flight to Miami, Florida. My schedule was to fly in on the thirty-first, go to the game that day, and take the train the next day. The thirty-first was the only other time my schedule was so tight. Thank goodness.

Got to Miami at 1:00 p.m. and took the shuttle to the hotel. Arrived at the hotel at 2:00 p.m. Checked in, changed into my Astros jersey, and took a bus to the ballpark. There wasn't much around the ballpark except one brand-new restaurant and bar that just opened today. It was 4:00 p.m. I had time for a bowl of soup and a beer. The menu was a very good one.

The gates opened at 5:30 p.m. The game was between the Marlins and the NY Mets. I was able to get four autographs and a baseball: #29 Ike Davis, first baseman for the Mets; #44 Jason Bay, outfielder for the Mets; #12 Scot Harrison, outfielder for the Mets; and #33 Mat Harvey, starting pitcher for the Mets. The game was only two hours and ten minutes—one of the fastest games ever played! The final score was Marlins 0, Mets 3.

I walked back to the sports bar I was at before and had a good dinner. Since it was so late, I took a cab back to the hotel. The weather was hot and humid—quite a contrast from Canada. Got back to the hotel and set the alarm for 5:00 a.m.

Saturday, September 1

I decided to take a cab to the Amtrak station. I couldn't find my hotel reservation for Tampa, Florida, so I called AAA. They gave me the info I needed. I'm at the Amtrak station now and writing in my journal. Got on the train at 10:30 a.m. There was a lady that got on and sat down next to me. She was in her sixties but in very good shape and condition. We had a lot of fun talking. Plus I had a flask of red wine that we shared. She reminded me of Joan Rivers in the way she talked and the way she sounded. She has lived in Florida for over twenty years but still had a very heavy Boston accent. It was a truly enjoyable five-hour trip. I have pictures.

I took a cab from the RR station to the hotel only because there was no other choice. Cost me $70. Got to the hotel at 6:00 p.m. and checked in. I walked around the area known as the pier with shops and restaurants, etc. Since I had a late lunch, I didn't feel like eating yet. I got on a trolley that went around parts of the city for only 25¢. I did buy a souvenir. I got off at an area full of bars, restaurants, and music but didn't go in. Got back on the trolley. I got off at a restaurant that looked very nice and overlooked the water. There was some outside seating. It was a beautiful night, so I sat outside. I finally ordered after 9:30 p.m. What I had was very good. I left there and walked around some more. I heard some singing and a band playing. It was out in the open and in a large courtyard. So I went over and sat down and listened to them for a long time. It must have been after midnight when I retired.

Sunday, September 2

This was a do-nothing lazy day. The weather was back in the nineties and humid. Back to shorts and short sleeves. Went to a Subway store and got a Footlong. I was able to mail a few things back to Houston. I kept trying to get on a small fishing charter but with no luck. I thought I had successfully booked a large fishing boat charter for Tuesday, September 4. So I went out and bought myself a nice small cooler that I would need. I did manage to write in my journal earlier. I had part of my sandwich at around 1:00 p.m. It's now well after 6:00 p.m. I went back out to a restaurant that specializes in oysters and seafood. It was after 10:30 p.m. when I made my way back to the hotel for the evening.

Monday, September 3

Stayed in until 10:00 a.m. and took the free shuttle to the ballpark at 11:00 a.m. It was a bit early, so I went to the only bar in the area and had a drink. I went in when the gates opened and went to where the Yankees were. I got the autographs from #14 Curtis Granderson, pitcher for NYYs; #48 Jim Hickey, pitching coach Tampa Bay Rays; #9 Elliot Johnson, infielder TB; and Rich Thompson, a outfielder for TB. The TB Rays won 4–3 over the Yankees.

It was after 4:30 p.m. Got back on the shuttle and got off on the street with many bars. I went back to a bar I had been before and had the baked oyster combo that was so good the other time. I made my way back to the hotel, poured myself a glass of wine, and lit a cigar and wrote in my journal. I got a call from the fishing charter.

Tuesday, September 4

I got a call from the fishing charter I was supposed to go on the next day, but it was canceled for lack of people. I spent the rest of the day sightseeing. There was really not much more for me to do here. This was probably the least active and most boring part of my whole trip. Good thing it came at almost the end of my trip. I did another load of laundry and had lunch at a tavern nearby.

Wednesday, September 5

Since my plans were changed and I'm leaving for Knoxville, Tennessee, on the sixth, I have one more day here. And since there is a game today, Tampa Bay versus New York Yankees, I will go to one more game tonight at 7:00 p.m. I hung around the hotel and snacked on some leftovers and a beer. I took the free shuttle to the ballpark and went to the only bar close by and had a drink. The gates opened at 5:30 p.m. I wore my jersey one more time. Again I was lucky and got autographs from #43 Steve Pearce, starting first baseman for the Yanks, and #19 Chris Stewart, catcher for the Yanks, and a lady broadcaster for the Yes TV station for the Yankees. I wasn't really into the game and since I got some autographs, I decided to go back to the bar and watch the game from there. I had something to eat and drink. The Yanks finally won a game 6–4 over the Rays. Got on the shuttle and walked back to the hotel. It was about 11:00 p.m. now. I finished packing and set my alarm for 5:00 a.m.

Thursday, September 6

Got going at 5:00 a.m. Got to the airport in plenty of time. The plane was supposed to leave at 10:40 a.m. We boarded the plane, and after sitting for about thirty minutes, we were told there was some mechanical trouble. After one and a half hours, we were able to leave. I called Delta to put me on a later flight out of Atlanta. It was a good thing I did because I would have missed my connecting flight to Knoxville. We got to Atlanta at 1:00 p.m. My flight was scheduled to leave at 3:00 p.m., so I had time to have lunch. When I got to my gate, the flight was delayed and took off at 6:00 p.m. It was only a forty-minute flight.

I had made reservations at a very nice hotel, convenient to everything. I called my friends here to let them know that I was in town. My timing was perfect for the few days I spent here. After getting settled, I went out at about 9:00 p.m. and walked to a Ruth's Chris Steak House very close by and had a very good and deserved dinner. I walked a little into town. The town was pretty much dead. I'm sure it's different on the weekends, especially during a football weekend. I walked back to the hotel and turned in.

Friday, September 7

Finally got up, got dressed, and went down to the lobby and got caught up with my journal. It's twelve noon. I went out to find a shirt and cap of the University of Tennessee Vols. Their colors were almost like UT's only a little different shade of orange. When I got to the store, I saw a very limited selection of things. I did find a good long-sleeved button-down shirt with pockets. It was the only one they had, so I bought it. I also bought a regular T-shirt and cap. I could wear the T-shirt under the other shirt. I knew I would need some cigars for the next day, so I was told where there was a good cigar shop. All this was in preparation for tomorrow's tailgating and game.

On the way back, I passed an old fort from the 1700s they had made into a museum. Also in the front was one of those wooden stockade things you put your arms and head through to be punished. So I got someone to take my picture in the stockade. When I got back to the hotel, I was able to use their computer and was able to print two pages from my journal.

I talked to James, the guy I met in St. Louis. He picked me up at 8:00 p.m., and we drove all around. We passed by the stadium also. Then we went to a casual but very good place to eat down on the Tennessee River. After dinner we walked along the river. You could see the back of the stadium from the river.

James is over six feet tall with a crew cut, a good build, good-looking with an eye for the ladies, and very smart. James explained to me that a large number of boats of all sizes, mostly very expensive ones, would be tied up there, and on the day of the game, there would be a lot more tied up. Some of them leave their boats tied up for the entire college season, and they lived on board. People would come from far and near. They would make a large contribution to that particular dock for that privilege. We walked around a bit more then we drove to an area called Old City. There were a lot of bars where the college kids hung out. They also had live music. We had a drink at two of them then I was dropped off at my hotel. I know it was after 1:00 a.m.

Saturday, September 8

The day of the big game has arrived. I got dressed in my new U of Tenn shirt and hat and went down to the lobby at 10:30 a.m. to write in my journal and wait for James to call. He picked me up close to noon. We drove to a parking lot that was out of the way of the stadium and would be easy to avoid the traffic. We had to walk quite a long way to get to where his friends were tailgating.

The tailgating site was an old abandoned drive-through bank. It was ideal because it provided some cover in case of bad weather, which came in very handy later. Also electric power for anything electrical such as TVs, computers, etc. They had a grill set up and going. Of course a good amount of beer and some whiskey and vodka if you wanted. People also brought things to eat and drink. About twenty to thirty people including some kids. Absolutely no shortage of anything.

I was introduced to his friends. There was a lot of joking among each other. To be expected. They threw me into the mix as well. Other tailgaters had tents set up. Some of them had a band. I walked over to a tent with a four-piece band. They were very friendly also and gave me a beer. Finally after a while, James's friend Camilla (the other person I met in St. Louis) joined us with a girlfriend of hers. It started to rain, so we moved everything undercover. Luckily, James bought two of those clear lightweight ponchos.

It was about 1:30 p.m., so we decided to walk to the second tailgating place. I lit up a cigar. That wasn't a good idea. I tried to keep it lit but couldn't. The second tent was a little more elaborate with more choices of food and drinks. There were tents set up on both sides and joined together. We stayed there until almost game time at 4:00 p.m. James and I had seats on the thirty yard line and under the grandstands, so we were protected from the rain. The girls had seats in the stands above us and were not protected from the rain.

I took some pictures at the tailgating and at the football game. It stopped raining before the game ended. U of Tenn won 51–13 over Georgia State. But they were supposed to win. The game was over at 7:00 p.m. We walked to a restaurant nearby that they knew of that was quite nice. We had a bite to eat and then James dropped me off at the hotel. It was close to 10:00 p.m. by then and I called it a day.

Sunday, September 9

Got up and went out at 9:30 a.m. Went down to the lobby to write in my journal for about an hour. I also typed out two more pages from my journal into the computer and printed it. I called James to get together with the two of them to watch an NFL game somewhere. They picked me up at about 1:00 p.m. We went to a really nice, which was about a four- or five-block square area—all cobblestone—only for pedestrians, with the middle area that had trees, benches, fountains, and large sculptures. The perimeter had shops, restaurants, and bars. They knew of a good place to eat and sit outside to dine. We had a good lunch and talked some more. They both had other things to do that afternoon. So they went on their way. I wanted to stay in that area and hang out. I watched the late afternoon game then went back to the Old City area and watched the Sunday night game from a bar and had dinner there as well. After the game was over, I went back to the hotel. It was after 10:30 p.m., and I was ready to call it a day. But what a day it was!

Monday, September 10

It was finally time to fly home. Probably a good thing but also a little bit regrettably. All good things must come to an end. The flight home was uneventful. I arrived in Houston at 5:00 p.m. My friend Moe picked me up at the airport. On the way home, he stopped to show me the three new kitchens he was working out of now and told me about the new schools he had acquired. I got back to my place after 7:00 p.m. I went first to get all my mail. Put my suitcases in my room but didn't unpack that night. I did sort out my mail, opened it all, and threw away the junk mail. I must have stayed up until almost 3:00 a.m. The next few days and months were spent catching up on things. It would have been helpful to be able to see pictures that I took and would have given you better idea of the different events I had on my trip.

In conclusion, as I look back on the trip and how almost perfect it was, it's hard to say if it could have been planned any better. It's the end of September, and I'm just now finished transferring my notes into the computer and printing them. There are a lot of people that would like to have a copy of it. I just might make it into a movie or a TV series. What do you think? I'm pretty sure that someone more experienced on computers could have planned the trip a lot faster and more efficiently than me. There were at least two places that I needed a few extra days before moving on to the next city. In California to see the wine country and in Baltimore to see my cousins Larry and Barbara in Delaware. In almost all the cities, I was able to experience their history, magnificent sights, and landmarks. So it was much more than a baseball tour. The only game I missed was the NY Mets. I will go back to NYC and complete the tour. Plus all the people who have invited me to see special events in their cities. Now I have to decide which pictures to use and frame. This will take me a few months and will be hard to do.

THE END

Trip to Myrtle Beach, South Carolina, April 12–17, 2013
Monday After the Masters (MAM), April 15, 2013

Friday, April 12

My flight left at 7:00 a.m. I booked Super Shuttle to pick me up at 4:30 a.m., which meant I had to get up before 4:00 a.m. I got to the airport in plenty of time, but I told the driver I was taking a United flight. So I was let off at Terminal C. The man at the curbside check-in informed me that I was on a US Airways flight that left from Terminal A. So I got on the train that took me to Terminal A. Got my boarding pass and went through security. I got to my gate thirty minutes before they started boarding. Then I made my connection to Myrtle Beach, South Carolina.

I decided to rent a car that I reserved the day before. I found my way to the North Beach Plantation Resort and got checked in. It was about 1:30 p.m. I told the bellboy that I needed a ticket to the Pro-Am Golf tournament on the fifteenth. He got me some numbers to call. I called one number and the man said he could get me a general admission ticket. So I told him it was fine. So he brought me the ticket at about 4:00 p.m. This was one of the two things I didn't have yet to complete my trip. The other thing was a pass or ticket to go to the Darius Rucker concert that same night (that was the big challenge).

After getting my ticket to the golf tourney, I decided to drive around a bit. The place I was staying was conveniently located to almost everything I needed to go to. I drove to the House of Blues where the concert was being held. I found out there was another concert that took place tonight. So I bought a ticket for that. I forgot to mention that I took in my suitcase two bottles of wine, one mag. of white and one mag. of red. The bottle of red broke. My unit was equipped with a washer and dryer. So I did two quick loads of wash. My unit was beautiful and very well equipped, with a balcony that looked out into the swimming pool and the beach and the Atlantic Ocean.

It's now about 6:30 p.m. I ate a very good but quick dinner at a very upscale steak house on the premises. Now it was about 8:30 p.m. and time to go to the first concert. The first group was excellent. The second group was not as good. I left the concert about 11:00 p.m. Before I left Houston, I made reservations to go diving on Saturday, the thirteenth, at 8:00 a.m. I neglected to bring a bathing suit and a pair of tight-fitting water shoes.

Saturday, April 13

I woke up at 5:30 a.m. and called the diving place and told them that I had to cancel for those reasons. After that, I went back to sleep and woke up again about three hours later. One more thing I forgot to mention was that it rained for about thirty minutes on late afternoon Friday. After that, it cooled down and was beautiful. I called a guy I had called before leaving Houston about getting on a fishing charter with him. He didn't have an opening for me yet.

It's now about 11:00 a.m., and I'm writing in my journal. Today it's clear and in the sixties and seventies. I'm going out shopping in a short time. I finished my shopping and found everything that

I needed. I'm on my balcony eating some leftovers from last night and a beer (sounds familiar?). I will go down to the beach and walk around a bit in search of—you guessed it—a stick. There was nothing on the beach but some tall thin twigs and grass. So I walked back a different way.

There was a construction site just across the street from the resort. Again I'm glad I didn't go diving this morning because the water was a bit cold. I located a good stick, but I had to go a little ways off the beaten trail, when I found myself surrounded by five or six bumblebees. So I stood very still and made very slow movements and picked up the stick.

While I was shopping, I also found two hats that I wanted. I wrapped the stick in some thick garbage bags and some tape I got from housekeeping earlier. I'm sitting on my balcony with a cigar and a beverage and writing in my journal and watching part of round three of the Masters. It's very relaxing here. The pool area is very active. There is a swim or walk-up bar, there are tables IN the water near the edge of the pool where one can put things on, there are at least four different pool areas, of course the usual lounge chairs, and at least two or three Jacuzzis (hot tubs). My balcony is in the shade, but that's OK with me. I just saw Tiger Woods double bogey the ninth hole. He is now at -1 and about seven off the lead. So much controversy about him and that dropped shot on the fifteenth hole on Friday.

There is a Darius Rucker concert I will be going to later on tonight. I went to a fantastic Italian restaurant before the concert. The concert was great. I got up as close as I could, standing in the middle of a mass of screaming people. I left the concert a little early because I was very tired. I got back to my unit and fell asleep on the couch watching TV. When I woke up, I went back to sleep in my bed.

Sunday, April 14

Woke up about 9:30 a.m. and did not leave my room or get dressed. Watched the Masters and the Comedy Central the whole day. So much for Sunday. Oh yes, I had some leftovers.

Monday, April 15

The big day. Woke up at 5:00 a.m. and watched *Mike & Mike in the Morning*, two guys that come on ESPN2 TV and radio from 5:00 a.m. CT to 9:00 a.m. CT. They talk about everything sports related and joke around a lot also. They are broadcasting today from the House of Blues as they always do on the Monday After the Masters. Heard them talk about it for a few years now and was the reason I came down here this year.

And what a day it was! I got to the <u>House of Blues</u> about 6:00 a.m. They were setup on the stage, sitting behind a longer than usual desk. There were about fifteen rows of chairs, about fifteen chairs per row on the main floor. There were three steps up to another level with a railing and people standing behind the railing that went all the way around with a bar at the back of that (but the bar wasn't open). There was also an upstairs level with a lot of people on the second level. Some of the people in the front rows had signs from the local college that would hold them up during the breaks.

During the brakes Mike Golick (the big one) would come down into the crowd and autograph whatever you had for him to sign. I had a new straw hat that he could sign on the inside of it on the sweat band. He made the comment, "That will wear off when you sweat." I replied, "I don't sweat." He gave me a LOOK as if to say oh yeah. I gave my hat to one of their assistants onstage to give my hat to the other Mike to sign and he did.

After the show was over, I took a small poster down off the wall with their names on it. I showed it to Mike Greenberg (the small one) to sign. But before he started to sign it, I mentioned that his hairstyle reminded me of Jerry Lewis's hairstyle. He thought I said he looked like Jerry Lewis and didn't like that remark at all and asked why I had to be nasty? I explained that I said his hairstyle was like Jerry Lewis's. He was ignoring me. I followed him around and made some sort of an apology. Then I said, "Be a mensch" because he was also Jewish. And he understood and signed the poster.

Then I went to line up to go on the shuttle that took us to the golf tourney. I was asking people if they had a ticket or a pass to get into the concert tonight. A man right in front of me had a VIP pass for the tourney and for the concert. I gladly paid him $150 with that VIP pass I could get into any place I wanted to at the tournament as well as the concert.

By this time it was about 11:00 a.m. A few nights earlier, I met a man who was well-known on that golf course that told me to look him up at the fourteenth green. He went by the name of TP. When I got off the bus, I walked to the clubhouse first. There was a large buffet set up and in another room was a complete bar. So I helped myself. On the outside in the front of the clubhouse, there were a large number of golf carts ready to take the players to the golf course. That's when I started to get some of my autographs on the front of my shirt.

After they all left like a mass exodus, I started walking to the different holes. I made it to the fourteenth green. You wouldn't believe it. There were about ten or more golf carts lined up facing the fairway. A bunch of chairs were lined up also facing the fairway. There was a sign that read Welcome to the Fourteenth Hole. There was a large number of older men and women socializing (eating, drinking, talking, just having a great time). Off to one side there was a small tent set up with two grills and someone grilling hamburgers and brats (large hot dogs) with all the trimming.

At the far back was someone's house with a bar set up on the front porch. I did find TP to say hello. He said to make myself at home so I did. As the different groups of golfers and celebrities made their way to the fourteenth fairway and stopped for their next shot at the ball, a few of us approached them to ask for their autographs. And because this was not a real tourney, they were very obliging and did sign. Here is the list of golf pros' autographs I got: Jim Furyk, John Daly, Dustin Johnson, D. J. Trahan, Mark Lye, Chris DiMarco, Tommy Carney, and Harold Varner. I got autographs from the following celebrities: Darius Rucker, Mike Golic, Wayne Gratzky (NHL legend—when he was passing through, someone mentioned that he would like a cigar, so I had an extra one, so I went over and gave him one. He looked surprised because most people are asking him for things), Jim Cantore (the Weather Channel), Michael Waltrip (NASCAR driver), Rick Berry (NBA Hall of Fame), Jim McMahon (QB Chicago Bears Super Bowl), Dan Marino (OB Miami Dolphins, HOF), and Johnny Damon (ex NYY, MLB). Seventeen signatures total. Not bad.

The tourney was over a little after 5:00 p.m. I made it back to my unit and am writing in my journal now. I will be going back out later to go to dinner and then go to the concert. I went to the same Italian restaurant I went to before that was so good. They served way too much food. So I took a doggie bag. Got to the HOBs where the concert was being held and made my way as close to the stage as possible. The concert was OK but not great. There was just not enough energy in their selection of songs, and Darius was not lively enough of a performer. But everyone around me was singing along and was into it. Must be the age. I left at about 10:00 p.m. Good news, I did get a call from the fishing charter that I was going out Tuesday morning at 7:00 a.m. I did get directions earlier. It's now about midnight. I left a wake-up call for 5:00 a.m. What a fantastic day!

Tuesday, April 16

Woke up at 5:00 a.m. The fishing charter leaves at 7:00 a.m. I found my way with no problem. It was a beautiful cool morning. I was glad I wore a light jacket. I also brought four beers. There were five other guys on the boat. All related somehow. The youngest was fourteen. There were three generations. When we got about five or six miles out, we dropped some lines and trolled for some bigger fish for about thirty minutes with no luck. We went out about two miles more and started bottom fishing. This proved to be very successful. Everyone was catching a lot of fish, including me. They were all too small to keep, so they released them. Got some good pictures. We headed back at 11:15 a.m. I did drink two beers. We got back in at noon. When I got back to my unit, I had some leftovers and relaxed. I was planning to go back out that evening but didn't.

Wednesday, April 17

Got up at 7:00 a.m. to catch my plane at 11:00 a.m. I needed to get to the airport a little earlier because of the heightened security level because of the Boston bombing on the fifteenth. Got on the plane, and we took off. In Charlotte, North Carolina, the plane was delayed over three hours coming in from Chicago. We left at about 5:00 p.m. We got into Houston at about 6:30 p.m. CT. My friend Moe was waiting for me. My stick made it in OK, but my suitcase cane was in another airline. So I had to go to the other terminal to get my bag. Finally got home after 9:00 p.m. A very long day.

I thought that I would make this a yearly tradition, but after the nearly perfect trip, I don't think I could duplicate it again. So once is enough.

That's it for now.

MLB All-Star Trip
Citi Field, NYC, 07-13-13 to 07-21-13

Saturday, 07-13-13

This is to give you an idea of how the very first part of my trip went. I set my alarm for 6:00 a.m. but failed to turn it on. Woke up at 5:30 a.m. Called United Airlines to reconfirm my reservation. Gave them all the info I had. They couldn't find my reservation. That's when I realized I was flying on Southwest Airlines. After that, the rest went well. I called them and all was in order. A lady friend of Moe's picked me up promptly at 6:30 a.m. (luckily, I called ahead to confirm my reservation) and took me to Hobby Airport. I went through the shortest security line ever.

I stopped at a bar and restaurant that was open and had my traditional Baileys and coffee. Boarded the plane. The flight was a full one. We landed in NYC about 3:40 p.m. ET. Caught the airport shuttle to the hotel. Got checked in and unpacked. Made some phone calls to people that I know and made contact with the agent I know that has all the tickets I needed for the All-Star packages. I also talked to the hotel concierge who gave me a lot of good info. I then went out to get a bite to eat at an Italian restaurant that the concierge had recommended and was close by and possibly a place where I could sit outside and smoke a cigar, which is illegal in New York. It's now about 10:30 p.m. when I returned to my hotel. Tomorrow is going to be the start of a very busy few days. The weather has been overcast and in the seventies.

Sunday, 07-14-13

I got started about 9:00 a.m., and I got directions on how to get to the convention center where the Fanfest for the All-Star game was being held. They were very easy directions going by subway. When I came up to the street, I turned the wrong way and walked about ten blocks the wrong way. But it turned out to be a good thing because I walked past the aircraft carrier *Intrepid* and took some incredible pictures of the incredible jet planes that were on board and the nuclear submarine next to it. I turned around and made my way back to the convention center about 10:30 a.m. I forgot to mention that I brought with me on the trip three small bottles of tequila, vodka, Crown Royal, a bottle of white wine, and a bottle of red wine and a plastic flask that fit perfectly in the front pocket of my shorts. Today I filled the flask with vodka and orange juice.

I got to the Fanfest and walked around at first. I went to the All-Star gift shop and bought the souvenirs that I wanted. At some point, I got a cup of ice and poured myself a drink from my flask. I didn't take part in some of the events like I did the year before. Instead I was more interested in getting the autographs of the Hall of Fame ballplayers to add on to my jersey that I wear. So I stood in line. The first one was of Turk Wendell, the famous relief pitcher for the NY Mets, and Juan Marichal, the ace pitcher for the San Francisco Giants. There were others, but I decided to leave at about 2:30 p.m.

Took the subway to Citi Field, the home of the New York Mets. The two events for today were the Futures game with the upcoming stars from the minor leagues and after the celebrity softball game between retired athletes and other famous people from TV, movies, and the current Miss America. It was very hot, and being surrounded by a huge number of people made it even worse. At all the All-Star events, it was impossible to get autographs because of all the media surrounding the players. So I settled back and watched the game. I did have a bite to eat at the game and another tall drink from my flask. It was definitely entertaining.

After the game, I made my way back to the hotel by subway with the help of a few people. When I got back to the hotel, I took a well-needed shower. It's about 9:30 p.m. now. I poured myself a large glass of wine, and this is what I'm doing now, writing in my journal, along with some leftovers from the other night. Tomorrow is the Home Run Derby at 8:00 p.m.

Monday, 07-15

Since there was nothing for me to do until about 4:00 p.m., I did nothing. At about 2:00 p.m., I got hungry, so I went out and bought a Subway sandwich and took it back to the room. At about 4:00 p.m., I got dressed and headed out for the stadium by subway. Got there about 5:00 p.m. Unfortunately, I forgot to bring my flask. It would have come in handy. I went down to the area that I was permitted to go, but as I mentioned, it was impossible to get an autograph. As I was wandering around, a man stopped me. He hosts a radio talk show in Boston. He recorded his interview with me. I gave him my card and asked him to please send me a copy of the recording of the interview.

I settled down on a very nice seat behind the third-base dugout. The Derby was also very entertaining with some monster home runs hit. It was over after 11:00 p.m. There was Yoenis Céspedes (outfielder for Oakland Athletics). He wasn't even elected to play in the ASG. On the way to catch the number 7 subway, they announced that the number 7 was out of order. The next option was the Long Island Rail Road (LIRR). Of course there were thousands of people trying to get on that train. A lot of people were very mad and almost started to tear the fence down. There were a lot of funny comments made.

After a long time they announced that that the number 7 was running again. So I got on the number 7 and made it back to the hotel after midnight, watched some TV, and went to sleep.

Tuesday, 07-16

Today is the ASG. It starts at about 8:00 p.m. I was told the gates open at 4:30 p.m. So I planned to be there at that time. I went up to the twelfth floor where there were some computers. That was where I've been printing my journal for the past few days instead of handwriting it. Went back up to my room and changed into my usual attire and took the subway to the ballpark. Since it is now a weekday and close to the rush hour, the subways were packed. I got to the ballpark just before they opened the gates. This time I didn't forget my flask. There were two guys in line with me that remembered seeing me at three different places. That has actually happened a few times. I guess because many of us have tickets to the same events.

I went down to the place that I thought I had the best chance for a ball or an autograph but no such luck. I got myself something to eat and a cup of ice for my drink. When I got settled in on a seat, a very attractive lady from the Dominican Republic sat next to me. She spoke just enough English for us to carry on a conversation. She didn't know too much about baseball, so I explained a little to her. I was lucky enough to stay there the whole game. The game by the way was a low-scoring one. The American League won 3–0. Mariano Rivera, NY Yankees's ace closing pitcher, came in to pitch the eighth inning. He got a standing ovation, and players from both leagues were standing in front of their dugouts. He retired the sides in order. Someone else came to pitch in the bottom of the ninth. There were some very good plays but overall not a very exciting game. American League got nine hits and the

National League got three hits. Mariano Rivera was voted the MVP of the ASG.

I am back at my hotel now. It is after 2:00 a.m. I'm on the first floor on a computer writing in my journal and calling it a night.

Wednesday, 07-17

Tonight I will meet with my friend Aja Zanova, the world figure skating champion and Olympic gold medal winner. We share the same birth dates and have been friends for a long time. We make it a point to call each other each year on our birthdays. And I have visited her when I've come to NYC. Since I had nothing to do until 5:00 p.m., that's what I did At 5:00 p.m., I got dressed and found out her apartment was only a few blocks away and didn't need a cab. I was very early, so I went into a drugstore and looked at some of the pictures I had taken. The machine I was on didn't allow me to do the things I wanted to do, so I will do them when I get back to Houston. I also had time to look through a Whole Foods–type store and saw a gigantic ostrich egg.

I got to her apartment on time at 6:30 p.m. She had the usual bottle of cold champagne and a selection of cheese. One of them was my favorite, the Saga Blue (a soft-style blue cheese). We had the usual conversation. And I showed her some pictures of my new granddaughter and some of the family. She also showed me some of her new awards and medals she has received from the president of the Czech Republic. One of them was being elected to the World Figure Skating Hall of Fame. Very impressive.

We finished the bottle of champagne and walked to the restaurant she wanted to take me. When we talked on the phone, before coming to NYC, we agreed that the restaurant she picked out didn't have to be the most exclusive restaurant in NYC since we had already done that. She chose a place that was owned from the same country that she was from, and as usual, she was very well-known there. The food was very good, and there was a nice crowd there for a Wednesday night. We had a very good dinner with a bottle of wine. My treat. We took a cab back to her place, and I walked back to the hotel.

Thursday, 07-18

Today I will meet with my cousin Joannie from New Jersey. We will see a Broadway show called *Wicked*. Today is the first round of the British Open played in Scotland. It is one of the major golf tournaments. I watched as much as possible on TV. It starts in the morning in the States. It's about 1:30 p.m., and I'm writing in my journal. Joannie and I will meet before the play for dinner at 6:00 p.m. at a very good restaurant right next to the theater that the concierge recommended at the hotel. I got dressed and left the hotel about 5:00 p.m. I took a cab this time to avoid the rush-hour crowds.

The restaurant was practically at the entrance of the theater. The restaurant was excellent. It was my treat of course. Joannie and I talked about things we were doing and everything in between. I showed her pictures that were still in my camera of the baby with the family, etc. She showed me some of her pictures and videos on her camera at different events. We each had a light dinner, and I had a glass of wine. We finished in perfect time. We got seated a few minutes before the play started. The seats I bought several months before were two rows from the stage, just about center. The name of the play was *Wicked*. It's a little hard to explain, but it's about the good witch and the bad witch in the *Wizard of Oz*. Very good acting, singing, clever lines, great effects—overall very entertaining. The show lasted two hours and forty-five minutes with a fifteen-minute intermission. That brought us out about 11:00 p.m.

Joannie took some pictures of me in front of some billboards. Then she went to catch her bus, and I went for a walk on Broadway toward Times Square. I was amazed at the number of people on the streets, but I guess I shouldn't have been. This was like a second show for me, seeing all the people and a good number of different cartoon characters that you could have your picture taken with if you wanted to and I did. The absolute best ones were not cartoon characters but two very beautiful, very well-built, exotic, and almost completely naked ladies with feathered fans. I couldn't resist! Their "manager" took the pictures with me in different poses for a nominal fee of $5 but well worth it. Even one of me on my knees between them.

After that I went to the famous restaurant Sardi's to have a bite to eat. To my surprise, the kitchen was closed, but the bar upstairs was open. So I went to the bar and had a drink. Sitting at the bar next to me were two people who were sitting next to Joannie and me at the restaurant. I finished my drink and took a cab back to the hotel. It was well after 2:00 a.m. I had part of a leftover sandwich and went to bed.

Friday, 07-19

It's after 9:00 a.m., and I'm writing in my journal. Today I will go back to Citi Field for the Mets game. I will wear my Astros jersey for the last time. When I get back, I will put it in a large frame and hang it up. I left the hotel about 4:00 p.m. and took the subway. I think that I have entered the subway station from four different locations to take the same two trains, and on the way back, I have exited at four different exits but always a block or so from the hotel. Anyhow, I got to the game at 5:00 p.m., just when the gates opened. I brought my flask with me again. Went down to the field to get some autographs when they announced that Rusty Staub, the ex–Houston Astros player, was signing autographs at a location in the stadium. This seemed like a much better opportunity.

When I got up to him, I introduced myself that I was from Maxim's and so on. He remembered it well and asked me if I wouldn't mind waiting awhile so that he could take some time to talk to me. He called for me to come back over, and we talked for a few minutes, and he signed my jersey. Then I went back down to the field level where I was able to get one more autograph from #9 Domonic Brown, left fielder for the Philadelphia Phillies and one of the 2013 All-Star players.

I didn't stay for the game (that ended 13–8 Phillies). Instead I went out to eat at a restaurant my friend Moe recommended that was inside the Hotel Pennsylvania, directly across from Madison Square Garden. The name of the bar was the Stelton Bar and Grill on the main level of the hotel. I sat at the bar like he told me. The bartender was very entertaining, and I also struck up a conversation with a man sitting next to me who was a regular there. I ordered a half dozen Blue Point oysters that were very good and a glass of chardonnay. Then I ordered the single lamb chops and the garlic mashed potatoes that Moe had recommended that were also very good with a glass of red wine. Talking with the people made the evening last a nice long time. I left there and took the subway back to the hotel about twelve midnight.

Saturday, 07-20

Got up to write in my journal after 10:00 a.m. I've been using their computers that were free each time. I will do some shopping for some things that I needed. Nothing much to do until tonight when I go out to eat and see another Broadway show that was a last-minute idea because Saturday was an open day. I got tickets for the show *Kinky Boots*, winner of six Tony Awards and highly recommended. This time the hotel concierge recommended a restaurant about four or five blocks from the hotel that specialized in seafood and steaks. The reservation was for 5:30 p.m. I headed out at 4:00 p.m. I did some shopping at a drugstore one block away and brought it back to the room. Then I saw a CVS close to the restaurant, so I succeeded in printing a few photos with some text on them.

I made it to the restaurant on time. I had a good amount of time to eat, and I was good and hungry. I started with some lightly seared peppered tuna, followed by a small cup of lobster bisque. The main course was seared sea bass and crème brûlée for dessert and three glasses of chardonnay. Got on the subway and made it to the theater in plenty of time. *Kinky Boots* is about an old outdated shoe company that was taken over by the son after the father passes away. It's up to the son to come up with new and innovative ideas to keep the shoe store in business. With the help of a transvestite and "his" friends, they succeed. There are a lot of inner plots and personal problems to overcome and they do. Great singing, dancing, acting, set designs, and a whole lot more.

Took the subway back to the hotel. I cleaned up some and did some packing and went down to the first-floor computers and wrote in my journal while it's still fresh in my mind and won't have to do it when I get back. It's after 12:30 a.m. now.

Sunday, 07-21

I fly back to Houston this morning. I get in at 3:30 p.m. I spend Monday, the twenty-second, in town and leave for Colombia on the twenty-third to meet up with my friend Moe for a week. But that's another story.

Trip to Bogotá and Cartagena, Colombia, 07-23-13 to 07-29-13
The Good, the Bad, and the Ugly

Tuesday, 07-23

First, the bad—I flew from Houston to San José, Costa Rica and from there to Bogotá, Colombia. Went through customs with no problems. Took a cab to the hostel that Moe had made reservations for the two of us. When I got to the hostel, they didn't have a room for me, and Moe was supposed to have been there already but didn't get his flight. He flew on standby. The lady took me to another hostel nearby. I guess I didn't fully understand what a hostel really meant. It was not agreeable at all. Moe was supposed to arrive earlier this morning but didn't make that flight either.

In Bogotá, it's in the forties and sixties. I was not prepared for the cold weather. I was trying to get another place to stay for just one night but to no avail. I also found out that our original destination was a town named Cali. Moe thought it was on the coast but it wasn't. My trips are usually located on the beaches.

Wednesday, 07-24

After I found out it wasn't, I spent the rest of the day at a travel agency changing my reservation to go to Cartagena, a city on the beach. After spending about at least five or six hours with the agency, I finally made all the necessary changes, including my spending one more night in Bogotá before leaving for Houston. It was now close to 4:00 p.m., and I hadn't eaten all day. There was a nice restaurant a block away on the second floor. I had a fairly good meal with some wine.

Second, the ugly—walking back to the hostel, I was almost there when I had a case of diarrhea. Yes, diarrhea. I almost made it back but just couldn't hold it back. I reached the hostel and went to my room to grab something I could wrap around me when I went to the room where the showers were. I was able to get out of my shorts and underwear and socks that couldn't be saved. I rinsed off and wrapped the thing I had with me around me and went to my room. You might wonder why I would write about that. It is all part of the trip and experience. The only thing that was OK was my shirt.

Moe was supposed to arrive late tonight. As far as I know, he didn't. There was so much confusion about the room. The lady put me up for the night in a room WITH a private bathroom at another location. I was glad about that. In Bogotá, everyone else was walking around in sweaters, long pants, and long-sleeved shirts except me.

Thursday, 07-25

I told the man at the front desk to wake me up at 5:00 a.m. I never got a call. I woke up at 5:30 a.m. Since I slept in my clothes and was already packed, all I had to do was to brush my teeth and hair and go. I got a cab for the airport. I made the plane in plenty of time. I got to Cartagena. EVERYTHING got better. This is the good part of the trip. Except when I unpacked I realized that I had left all my toiletries behind. But they were easily replaced. I did go out and buy the things I needed and a cap with Cartagena on it. Also, I had a diving charter for Friday, the twenty-sixth.

The hotel I was staying at wasn't helpful. I went into a nicer, bigger hotel that has a travel agency desk. She was able to get me on a diving charter on Friday, the twenty-sixth. I will have a cab take me to the diving store at 7:30 a.m. By the way, the weather here was in the nineties. Also by the way, I'm now wearing the necklace with all the shells on it, and I'm sure it is my good luck charm.

I went to another upscale hotel to see if they could find me a fishing charter. For some reason they don't have many or any of those here. What a business opportunity. After no luck, it was time to hit the beach and walk around. My hotel was about three blocks from the beach. As I was walking on the beach, two guys approached me as a lot of them do. We talked a while and the conversation turned to fishing. With my limited Spanish and their limited English, I was able to book a fishing charter with them. I tried to make myself as clear as possible. I was very curious to see what they would come up with. This is for Saturday, the twenty-seventh, early in the morning.

I continued my walk on the beach, now in search of a walking stick. After quite a long walk in both directions I found a real good one. It was about three feet too long. So I took it to one of the bar huts where they served the coconut drinks. They had to have a large knife to cut the coconuts. So I asked the barman if he would cut off part of the stick. So he did. I offered him a tip, but he refused so I bought a coconut drink (which I needed by now). After I finished it, I gave him a good tip. So now I have gotten all the things I came here for, and if I wanted anything else, it would have been easy to get!

As I was walking on the beach, two beautiful young ladies passed me going the other way. I looked back, and one of them was looking back at me. So we got together and talked for a while. I had someone take a few pictures of us for show. And that was as far as that went. It could have developed even further, but I wasn't interested at the time. So far, what a turnaround from Bogotá, and it gets better.

I think Moe continued on to Cali as he had planned. It felt good to be in a hotel with all the modern conveniences. In one day, I accomplished all the things I needed. It will be interesting to see how the diving and fishing turn out. I went back to the hotel and took a shower and got the sand out of the shoes and socks I was wearing. I went out to a restaurant nearby. It was sort of an Italian cuisine. I had a good dinner and a bottle of wine. I brought my journal with me when I went back out. So I took my time writing in my journal with the wine and eating. I hadn't written in my journal in a long time, so there was a lot to remember. Earlier in the day, I took my first ass picture. It was one of the best ass shots of two women ever. It is now after 10:30 p.m. I went back to the hotel and finished the bottle of wine.

Friday, 07-26

Woke up at 6:30 a.m., got dressed, went downstairs, and waited for the cab I arranged to take me to the diving place. I arrived at 7:00 a.m. One of the dive masters was a very pretty lady. The others were getting all the tanks and other gear ready for the dive. She helped me get the right-sized flippers and fill out the paperwork. When the gear was ready, they loaded it into the van and took it to the diving boat then came back for me. There were eleven of us on this dive. Some of them were native Colombians but lived in the United States now. They had some other relatives here with them. There was a young couple from Tennessee. Everyone spoke English. It was a good group. The weather was ideal. The water was good and calm.

The first dive was around a shipwreck. We saw lots of different fish, but nothing very big. We did see a squid. The dive lasted about forty to forty-five minutes, which is the normal length of time. After that dive, we all got into the boat and motored over to a beach where we all had a bite to eat and some juice. We also had some water the first thing we all got back into the boat. We took the usual one-and-a-half-hour break then headed back out for our second dive.

It's now about 11:00 a.m. We all had been paired up with a dive master. There were three of us for one dive master. This was very agreeable. The second dive wasn't as good as the first one. There was a little stronger current. We did see some larger fish. One of the ladies said she saw a very large lobster. There were two of the women who were young, well-built, and good-looking. I took pictures of the entire gang before the first dive and after the dive was over. We were all tired, hungry, and thirsty.

Got back to the hotel, took a shower, and changed. Went out about 3:45 p.m. and bought a six-pack of beer for the fishing trip tomorrow. The weather was turning a little overcast but still nice.

I stopped for a small snack and continued my walk on the beach. I put sunblock on for the first time that I'm here in Colombia. I enjoyed more than one coconut drink while I was on my walk. I saw the people who will take me out fishing, and I wanted to make it perfectly clear (as clear as possible) that we were on the same page. I think we were. They asked for some money in advance, but I told them NO. And we understood how much I was going to pay.

I stopped for a quick dinner and wrote in my journal. It's about 7:30 p.m., and I joined back up with my new friends in front of the bar hut, and we sat down and had a few drinks and talked. It was a beautiful evening. While sitting with my new friends that evening, I asked him for the hat he had on. I told him I have a collection of hats, so he gave it to me. The hat is from España (Spain). Very special. In the next two days I was given two more caps from other guys (cool). We sat there for a good long time, drinking and talking. I was introduced to a variety of people who sat down and talked with us, including a gynecologist. There were some good jokes told. It was quite late when we called it a night. I went back to the hotel.

Saturday, 07-27

Today is the day I go fishing. It is about 5:00 a.m., and I'm writing in my journal before going fishing. I met them at 7:00 a.m. When I first saw the boat, I wasn't too thrilled. It was about one and a half size larger than a rowboat with a fifteen-hour power motor. The man I booked the charter with and another man to steer the boat, who by the way had a half of an arm and a good arm, they didn't have rods and reels but spools of line. I know that none of this sounds good, and I was tempted not to go, but there really wasn't much of a choice if I wanted to go fishing at all.

And it turned out extremely well. We went out a few miles before we started to troll. We trolled (fishing on the surface of the water at a slower speed) for about forty minutes and caught about five or six nice fish. Then we went to a different place and fished near the bottom. The water was calm with only two- to three-foot swells. The weather was overcast, and it rained ever so slightly and stopped after a short time. I (we) caught about twelve to fifteen more fish. Some were good-sized fish. Of course I have pictures of most of them.

As we headed in, we trolled for a little longer and caught about five more fish. During the time of fishing, I drank three beers. When we started back in, the two guys each had a beer. When we got the boat back on the beach and unloaded the cooler of fish, a large crowd gathered around to see all the fish we had caught. We lined them all up on a round wooden spool, and I took a lot of pictures of the fish and of the two guys. The man with half an arm could do more than most people with two good arms. They started cleaning the fish, and that took over one hour. I brought some baby pork ribs with me that I ate and a beer while they finished cleaning the fish. The plan was to cook some of the fish on a grill later that evening on the beach at about 6:30 or 7:00 p.m. I wanted to bring some white wine.

I went back to the hotel, took a shower, and changed and went back out. I took a cab to the old town of Cartagena to an old fortress where they filmed part of the movie *Romancing the Stone* with Michael Douglas and took some pictures. I walked around a bit and took a cab back. I told the cab driver to let me off at a grocery store that I have been to before and bought the wine for the fish fest later, then walked a few blocks back to the hotel. I put the wine into the small refrigerator in the room. There was about two hours before the party started.

I went back to the beach and sat and talked some more with my friends. One of them gave me his cap and another guy brought me a cap with the Colombian flag colors on it. I bought one cap and was given three. In the meantime, there was a very pretty young lady of twenty-three sitting by herself at the bar. So I invited her over to join us. She sat for a while and then went into the water. Before she got to the water, I took a picture of her from behind. She came out and sat back down with us. They were starting to get the fish ready to be grilled. I went back to the hotel for the wine and came right back. I had already opened them, and they were good and cold. I was given a few cups for a few of us. They also kept the other bottles cold. The fish were prepared with some sliced onions, tomatoes, fresh garlic, some olive oil, and a little white wine. Then wrapped in foil and put on the grill. When they were done, they brought them to the table, and I was served a very nice red fish with some fried potatoes. Of course, the fish was excellent. A few other people took part. All of us finished the three bottles of wine. It was a beautiful night on the beach. It was about 10:30 p.m. I couldn't talk the young lady to come back to the room with me except for a price that was much too much. Alone again.

Sunday, 07-28

I got up at 6:00 a.m., packed, and took a cab to the airport. I went back to Bogotá for only one night because my flight to Houston left on the twenty-ninth. I took a shuttle cab to the hotel. The hotel was only ten minutes from the airport. The weather here was back in the forties to sixties and cloudy. It was about 2:00 p.m. when I went out for a bite to eat. I really didn't eat very much because I was starting to get a little chilly. I went back to the hotel, put a blanket on the bed, took two Advils, and went to bed. I woke up a 6:00 p.m. feeling much better and hungry. The hotel has a restaurant on the second floor. They were just opening. I had some good soup and a main course with some wine. While I was eating, Moe called me and told me that the change that I made was not in his budget. There was a free shuttle service from the hotel back to the airport that I will take at 6:00 a.m. After dinner, I went back to my room, watched some TV, and went to sleep.

Monday, 07-29

I leave to go back to Houston today. My flight leaves at 8:11 a.m. Got the shuttle to the airport, checked in, went through security, and made the plane with no problems. We stopped in San José, Costa Rica. Had about a two-hour layover. Had a small snack and a glass of wine. I was checked through to Houston. Landed in Houston about 4:30 p.m. It took some time to get the bag and my stick and go through customs. Ron was waiting for me when I came out. Needless to say, it was good to be back home, and the absolute best time was spent in Cartagena! I was so glad I changed my plans. My next trip will be after the twenty-fifth of December, over NYE. Don't know where yet. To be announced.

Dove Hunting Trip
Lake Brownwood, Texas
09-16 to 09-18-13

Sunday, September 15

Drove from Houston to the town of Brownwood, Texas. Left Houston at 6:00 p.m. Arrived in Brownwood, Texas, at 11:00 p.m. Stayed at the Value Lodge overnight. This was the perfect thing to do.

Monday, September 16

Instead of getting up at 6:00 a.m., I had a good night's sleep and drove to the hunting lodge. Arrived at 10:00 a.m. and got all the paperwork out of the way early and a three-day hunting license. Most of the other guys arrived between 12:00 and 1:00 p.m. The ones that were already there sat around and talked. I had a beer and so did some of the others. These guys were totally prepared because they had hunted here before.

Lunch was at 1:30 p.m. After lunch, we all gathered under a group of trees and talked about a lot of stuff and had some more to drink. There was no shortage of alcohol around these guys, and they did enjoy their beverages. One was not supposed to drink before hunting, but that didn't stop them. They all could handle their alcohol very well. I was in very good company it seems.

There were several groups from different areas of the United States. They knew one another well. That made for some very amusing conversations and remarks the whole time we were there. Everyone got along very well. Some great stories, great BS as well. They ranged in ages from midtwenties and up. NO ONE was excluded from being ribbed. At 3:00 p.m., we headed out. There were about five or six vehicles following the main truck. About twenty to twenty-five of us at this one field. We were let off at about thirty- to fifty-yard intervals in hopes we would not shoot one another. It seemed to work.

By the time we got to the field and let off, it was about 4:00 p.m. The doves started flying shortly after. In a few minutes, it sounded like a war zone. One of the guys had a bird dog with him. The hunt lasted until 7:00 p.m. It was almost like the doves stopped flying at that exact time, like someone blew a whistle and it was quitting time for the doves. The wagon that dropped us off came by and picked us up. When we got back to the field entrance before heading back to the lodge, we had a few drinks and a cigar. One of the guys had a LARGE cooler in the back of his truck with a very good supply of alcohol and mixers. At about 8:00 p.m., we headed back to the lodge. At 8:30 p.m., we had dinner. It was buffet style. All sorts of salads, pot roast this night, a large selection of sides, jalapeno corn bread, and dessert was brought around a little later by the staff. Oh yes, there was an open bar and the bartender was very generous with her pours. It was Monday, and there was a TV with the Monday night football game on. I remember watching part of it and woke up at midnight and going back to my room. Each of the guys shared a room, but I was by myself in a room.

Tuesday, September 17

Next morning, while the others were on the shooting range for some kind of shooting competition, I went into town and filled up the car with gas, went to a liquor store, bought a pint of 1800 gold tequila, and some Macanudo cigars to share with the guys. Before lunch, I did a quick cleaning of my shotgun. We had lunch at 1:00 p.m.—salads, fried catfish, a lot of sides, breads, etc., and dessert if you wanted. We sat under the trees again with more of the same BS and drinks.

At 2:45 p.m., the same group headed out for another field. It was a little farther out this time. We all got in the back of a wagon just like the first time and were let off in spaces. I didn't like where I was, so after thirty minutes, the main man comes by, and I asked to be relocated. This was a much better spot but didn't improve my shooting. The first day I got two doves; this day I got three doves.

Again at 7:00 p.m., we were all gathered up and brought back to the field entrance. There were some peel 'em shrimps and red sauce and drinks and cigars to be had. Got back to the lodge and had dinner and open bar. I went to my room at about 10:30 p.m. and called it a night.

Wednesday, September 18

Got up, took my only shower, got dressed, packed, and went to the dining room to say good-bye and collect my doves. They divided all the doves equally for everyone. That was good for me. Left at about 10:00 a.m., got into Houston about 3:00 p.m. One fun trip.

Trip to New Orleans
September 27 to October 1, 2013

Friday, September 27

Picked up by Ron and Megan and taken to Hobby Airport. Got there in plenty of time to have a small lunch and a glass of wine. Boarded the plane at 2:00 p.m. Landed in New Orleans shortly after 3:00 p.m. Took a shuttle to the Hotel Royal in the lower French Quarters and got checked in. One of the purposes of my trip was to visit a bar by the name of Spitfire owned by Amanda, the daughter of a long-time friend of mine. Amanda and another lady, Sarah, are the owners. That's about as much explanation as is needed at this time.

I walked to the bar from my hotel. On the way to the bar, I bought a New Orleans Saints cap and a pair of sunglasses. It's about 6:00 p.m. now. Sarah was tending the bar. I took some notes before going in. I sat at the bar, and we started talking. I didn't tell her who I was, but she recognized my voice from talking to her on the phone. Amanda is in Lake Charles now and doesn't take much interest in the operation. After talking for a good length of time, I walked back to the hotel. Called my friend, Debbie, the mother of Amanda. She lived about two blocks from the hotel. She had a friend staying with her, a beautiful lady, maybe in her midthirties, by the name of Amber—a real hottie.

We sat on the steps of the doorway known as the stoop. Debbie made a cushion covered with a fabric and fit perfectly in the stoop. The three of us had some wine and talked about old times at Maxim's and so much more. While sitting on the stoop, an incredible amount of people passed by. Some of them stopped and talked to us. They were a lot of fun and very funny. It was now close to 9:00 p.m., and we went out for dinner at a nice restaurant nearby. We got back to her place and had some more wine and sat on the stoop and talked some more. The hottie went to sleep on the couch. We talked till about 2:00 a.m. I walked back to the hotel and went to sleep.

Saturday, September 28

I had a good night's sleep. Got up at about 10:00 a.m. I missed several calls because my phone was put on vibrate accidentally. Got dressed and went over to Debbie's place. The hottie, Amber, was at a yoga class. Debbie and I went grocery shopping. I picked out five bottles of wine for us to drink for later. Two Macon white Burgundies, a red Burgundy pinot noir, a good red Bordeaux, and a Reserve Shiraz from Australia. When we got back to her place, she put things away, and I sat down on the stoop with a glass of wine while Debbie put things away and started to prepare some snacks for the three of us for later, such as some pâté, some assorted cheeses, queso with some spicy sausage in it, crackers, bread, and chips.

Many people passed by. One man asked if he could come inside and look at the barstools. Then about six or seven guys dressed in Mardi Gras attire with very large round beads around their necks, funny clothing, and hats passed by. I couldn't resist stopping them and talking to them and having my picture taken with them. After that was when I decided to start my journal. Amber came back from her yoga class shortly after that. That's when we stopped for lunch and some wine. It was also about the time the Louisiana State University versus Georgia College football game came on

TV. It was a good game. LSU was ahead until the last five minutes of the game when Georgia scored again to win 44–41.

Amber and I must have dozed off for about an hour sitting on the couch. We also were waiting for Amber's sister and some friends to drop by after they finished with a play they had gone to. When they arrived, it was about 9:30 p.m. We talked about a lot of things, and at about 11:00 p.m., we went our separate ways. I went back to the hotel and got a box of leftovers from lunch I had at the airport in Houston. It was still good. Oh yes, when I first got to the hotel, they tried to put me in a room on the fifth floor with NO elevator. This was unacceptable. They were able to move me to the ground floor.

Sunday, 09/29/13

It's about 9:30 a.m. I got dressed and sat in the courtyard of the hotel with a cup of Louisiana coffee, writing in my journal. I'm going to Debbie's place now. We are going to a Sunday mass at the St. Jude's Church. I'm told it is 70 percent black and will get very lively. More on that later.

At Debbie's place, I had some coffee and talked for a while about our meeting with Sarah, the other partner in the Spitfire bar. Debbie mentioned several things that needed to be fixed or attended to. We are meeting with Sarah for lunch on Monday. I will write about that meeting later.

It was time to go to church. We got there just in time to find seats for the three of us. The church was full with people standing in the back. Shortly after the services started, a six-piece band took their places—a guitar, a piano, a drummer, a saxophone, two trumpets, and two black ladies that took turns singing. You can only imagine. There was one priest that conducted most of the service along with one or two others. All during the service, the band would play, and it did get livelier. People were standing and clapping their hands. This was amazing and enjoyable. NO, I'm not converting.

The sermon was quite good, and they passed the collection basket. I gave $10. The whole thing lasted about one hour. Debbie walked back to her place and started preparing lunch, while Amber and I stopped at a bar just to see what it was like to compare with Spitfire. Most bars that served food were the most successful. That was one of the issues with Spitfire. They will eventually get taken care of. I ordered a drink and took it with me.

We then went to a small grocery store to pick up some things for appetizers. I got another bottle of wine, some smoked salmon, an onion, some pumpernickel bread, and Amber bought a few things. We also stopped at two other stores that were of interest to Amber. We got back to Debbie's place. I put the wine in the fridge to get cold and chopped the onion for the smoked salmon. Amber put out some other things.

We had some very nice hors d'oeuvres before lunch. It was about 2:30 p.m. when the stuffed chicken was ready. Debbie sliced up the chicken, and we helped ourselves. We sat outside at her courtyard. Since we finished the white wine, we started on the red Bordeaux. We also were watching some of the pro football games. I guess some time after dark, we walked to Spitfire. Somewhere along the way, we picked up two strangers for no real reason, and they followed us to the bar. We had a few drinks and a lot of conversation. I'm guessing it was after 11:00 p.m. now. We stopped at the famous Café Du Monde. I bought one of their paper hats that they wear. Got back to the hotel and went to sleep.

Monday, 09-30-13

I got up about 10:30 a.m. Called Debbie to find out what was on the schedule. Her friend Amber left earlier. It's 11:00 a.m. I'm sitting in the lobby writing in my journal because it was ever so slightly. Debbie and I are meeting with Sarah at 1:00 p.m. at a restaurant to talk about the bar. Later on, I'm going to the Monday night football game between the Saints and the Miami Dolphins. Both teams are 3 and 0. Speaking about the Saints, at the end of the church services, they played "When the Saints Go Marching In."

It must have rained earlier this morning. The sky was very overcast but not dark. I'm going out now and walk around a bit before meeting with Debbie and Sarah at 1:00 p.m. I walked to an area known as the French Market. Sort of a five- or six-block-long cover of small open shops with almost everything you could imagine. But very many of the same type of shops. I was looking for some sort of unique belt made of leather. But there was no such shop that specialized in belts or buckles. What a great idea for a shop to have all kinds of belts and buckles. It would be the only shop of its kind in the market. I still had a lot of time before meeting with Debbie and Sarah at 1:00 p.m. The Mississippi River was close by, so I walked to the banks. On some rocks close to the water's edge, I saw some driftwood. By accident, one of them happened to be perfect for a walking stick. So I reached down and picked it up. Took it back to the hotel and got two large trash bags and some tape and wrapped it to take back with me on the plane.

By the time I got back to the restaurant, it was 1:00 p.m. We all got there at the same time. Again the reason for the meeting was to talk about what could be done to improve the bar operation and the business. There were a great number of things that need to be taken care of, but Sarah was taking care of them slowly she said. And Debbie's daughter, Amanda, was not around at all to help. We had about a two-and-a-half-hour lunch and discussed mostly all this. I don't think anything was accomplished.

Sarah was given a ticket to the Budweiser tailgating booth. So I followed her back to the bar and she gave it to me. I took a cab to the address of the tailgating that was about four blocks away from the dome. It started at 4:00 p.m. till 7:00 p.m. It was a shame that

I had eaten at such a short time before because they had some good food and plenty of beer. It started to rain ever so slightly but only for a few minutes. I took some pictures of some wild and crazy-dressed people. I left to go to the game at 6:00 p.m. I should have planned better and brought a flask with me. It would have been easy to bring it into the stadium. Next time, I will know.

The seat I had was in the end zone and way up at the top. The place filled up shortly after I got there. The people around me introduced themselves to me. This wouldn't happen in Houston. The home field advantage does make a big difference in New Orleans. Noise you couldn't believe. I took some pictures of some of the fans. People were high-fiving on any good play. Even on a five-yard gain by the Saints or a bad play by the other team. I left the game in the fourth quarter with about eight and a half minutes to go. The score was Saints 38, Miami 17. That was the score at the end of the game.

Everyone was doing the same thing. I was just following the crowd and ended up in the French Quarter on Bourbon Street. I found a bar that was still open and served food. I had a bowl of soup and some hot wings and some wine and a cigar. I know it was well past 1:00 a.m. when I left the bar. There were some people on some balconies throwing some beads, but they were nothing special, so I didn't bother. Went to the hotel and went to sleep.

Tuesday, October 1

Got up at 10:30 a.m., dressed, packed, and checked out. Sat in the lobby to write my journal. I left my bags there and went out. I went to one bar and listened to a pianist play some jazz and had a drink. Then went to a restaurant, Desire Oyster Bar, for a quick lunch. I had been there a few times before. Went back to the hotel and caught the shuttle for the airport. Arrived in Houston about 5:30 p.m. Was picked up by a friend. After unpacking and doing a few other things, I finished writing my journal. I'm pretty sure I will go back to New Orleans sooner than later.

Trip to Australia
December 26, 2013 to January 17, 2014

Thursday, December 26

Picked up by Ron at 1:00 p.m. Driven to the airport. Got there about three hours before the flight left from Terminal E. Went to the Pappadeaux restaurant very close to my gate. I ordered a half dozen raw oysters, but not from the Gulf of Mexico, and a glass of wine. Had a conversation with a couple on their way to New Orleans from Las Vegas. It was time to board the plane now. Of all things, the Alabama football team was on the same plane as me, heading to Los Angeles. They were playing in the Rose Bowl on January 1, New Year's Day. Did not see the coach, and I didn't make any remarks about them losing to Auburn.

We landed in Los Angeles about 7:00 p.m. In Los Angeles temperature was about seventy degrees. Got my next boarding pass to Brisbane. On the flight from Los Angeles to Brisbane, I watched three or four movies, three TV sitcoms, a TV news report, and some of the flight info, flight path, distance, etc.

My final destination was Cairns (the *r* is silent). The plane from Los Angeles to Australia was as big as Air Force One. It held 380 in total. We left Los Angeles on the twenty-sixth and arrived in Australia on the twenty-eighth because we passed through the international date line. I really don't know how that works and don't even bother trying to explain. I brought with me some black-eyed peas and cabbage for NYE, but customs didn't let me take the black-eyed peas in but the cabbage and the Bloody Mary mix was OK. I looked all over for some black-eyed peas to have before New Year's Day but none to be found. Arrived in Cairns about twelve noon.

Saturday, December 28

The weather in Cairns was in the nineties. It was hotter than usual. After I checked in and got settled, I went back down and inquired about a few things with the concierge. In Australia, they drive on the opposite side of the street. I'm glad I'm not renting a car. On that same note, you have to look to your right first before crossing the street. The Great Barrier Reef (GBR) is in Cairns and is not included on my tour. So I had to book it right away. The concierge was very helpful. I booked my dive for the morning of the thirty-first and later that night was NYE. I wanted to get that out of the way because you can't fly for twenty-four hours after your dive. I needed to buy two more pairs of short pants and three more short-sleeved shirts and go to a liquor store for some beers, some rum, and some juices.

It was about 1:30 p.m. now, and I hadn't eaten yet. So I saw a nice hotel with a nice restaurant in it. Because the store I was going to only opened at 4:00 p.m., I went to the liquor store first, took the stuff back to my room, and went back out. The store was open now, and I found everything I needed plus a very good-looking leather *Crocodile Dundee*–style hat with crocodile teeth in the front. It's a little like a cowboy hat but not. The hat was a great hit with people as will be told later.

On my way, I passed a jazz bar with an authentic Scottish band consisting of three guitars, a banjo, some sort of drum but not at all like you would imagine, a fiddle, and a piccolo player. There was a lady that sang but was not part of the band. She knew all the words to the songs they were playing. Took some great pictures and with me strumming on the banjo. At 7:00 p.m., a four-piece jazz group came in with the typical jazz instruments. I listened to them for a while and went to a nice hotel restaurant nearby and had a little dinner and went to bed.

Sunday, December 29

It's about 4:00 a.m., and I'm finishing today's journal. My first planned tour was by boat to the GBR. I took a good shower and felt refreshed. Back to short pants and short sleeves. I was early to be picked up by the bus, so I walked around a bit for about an hour. I saw one tree that was full of brightly colored parrots. I took a few pictures. I hope they come out OK. I walked a little farther and saw a tree full of bats—yes, bats—hanging upside down. Also took pictures.

Got picked up just outside the hotel and bused to the harbor terminal to board a large boat that took us first to a place called Green Island. We dropped off a few people that were going to spend the day there and picked them up on the way back. The rest of us went on to the GBR. The trip took about two hours. Once we got under way, the breeze felt good. I knew that I was going to do some snorkeling, so I wore my bathing suit. I sat up on the top deck of the boat and sat next to a husband and wife from London. Before I got settled, I got a double glass of white wine.

The couple and I talked about a lot of things. When we got to the GBR, we were given some instructions and some options. I chose snorkeling. We had a certain amount of time. We were given a special wet suit to wear to protect us from stingrays. I floated (swam) around for a good amount of time and took some incredible pictures with my new waterproof camera. Got back on the boat and had some lunch and another glass of red wine this time. Went back up to the top deck and enjoyed the sun. I was sitting next to a young lady from NYC. I took a picture of her. Her name was Daniel, the same name as my niece. We talked the entire time back to the terminal.

I was bused back to the hotel and changed. Went back out to the jazz bar. Sat down next to two ladies. Ordered the dirty martini I felt like having. The two ladies were a lot of fun to talk to. They taught me some Australian slang words and some other not-so-important facts. Walked back to the hotel. Got the leftovers from the other night, had them heated up, went back to my room, and had dinner and went to bed.

Monday, December 30

It's about 5:00 a.m., and by accident, I found the Sunday afternoon NFL game on TV while I'm writing in my journal. Today my tour will take me to a rain forest and other sites. I got dressed and went down for breakfast. I bought a few more souvenirs. I have not smoked a cigar yet but soon. Got on the bus at 8:45 a.m. Arrived at the first area about thirty minutes later. We were divided into two groups. This part of the tour showed and explained in detail all about the Aborigines' customs, rituals, dances, weapons, musical instruments, food, and more. The people that demonstrated all this were authentic Aborigines. Each one of the shows and demonstrations were very good. We were able to throw a boomerang. They made it look so simple but it wasn't. Mine didn't come back. After that, we were shown how to throw a spear. I think everyone got a few laughs out of watching one another. Took a lot of pictures. After that, we moved over to a sky rail that took us up and over the rain forest. I got off to walk around two times and got back on. The rail ended up in a small town. It was 1:30 p.m. now. We were given a few options. I chose to have lunch at the local hotel here.

There was a river that I walked down to. From the sky rail, one could see the falls by the name of Barron Falls, which was quite impressive. At 3:30 p.m., we were scheduled to go back by train. The train was delayed about an hour because there was an accident on the tracks involving a car that had to be moved. I think because it was so hot and on a little of a downhill trip, the train went extremely slow. There were trees on both sides of the tracks, so it was impossible to see much. It was a slow torturous trip down to where we caught the buses back to town.

When I got back to the hotel, I signed up for the ultimate NYE party bus I had heard about. I went to pick up my ticket in advance. Got back to my hotel about 9:30 p.m. Made some preparations for my dive on the thirty-first and went to bed.

Tuesday, December 31

It's now about 5:30 a.m., and I'm writing in my journal. So far I've been very lucky with the weather but might run into some rain later. Going to dive at the GBR today. Was picked up at 7:30 a.m. and bused to the boat. The boat was named *Reef Experience*—a very large boat. The main deck was enclosed with tables and seats near the windows and other seating in the middle. A small prep area in the middle for food and drinks. I brought a change of clothes, a towel, and three beers.

We were handed some forms to fill out when we boarded—the regular info about diving and other things. We were given a wet suit, fins, and a mask. We were all given a group number, about four people to a group. We were given the rest of the gear when it was time for us to dive. I gave my beers to one of the guys in the prep area to keep cold for me. I was sitting next to a nice couple from Oregon. They were only going to snorkel.

The crew went over the dos and don'ts and rules. They served a breakfast sandwich, but I didn't have any. There was an upscale diving package offered, but I was too late to sign up for that. As it turned out, the upscale diving package was nothing special. After a while, I decided to explore and went upstairs to the sundeck. It was very comfortable. I stayed there for a while. Before we got to the reef, my name was called out to let me meet the other people and the dive master. A nice small group. It was time to do our first dive. We were helped on with the rest of our gear.

After we were in the water, we started to descend. Everything was working fine. My problem, as it has been in the past, was not being able to go up or down or stay horizontal when I needed to. The dive master helped me often. I was able to keep up with the others and looked around a lot and took some pictures also. We all stayed down for about forty-five minutes, which was normal. It was beautiful but didn't see anything out of the ordinary. There was also a professional photographer taking pictures of all of us. There was a natural bridge underwater that we went through. We only went about fifty feet down. That was the maximum for my camera. The whole experience was OK but not great. When I got back on board and handed in all my gear, I decided not to take the second dive. The dive started at 10:00 a.m. and ended a little before 11:00 a.m. I went up to the sundeck and dried off. I brought a change of clothes but didn't need them. Put on some more sunblock and sat outside for a while. There was a man grilling some sausages on the top deck. It sure smelled good. Since I wasn't going back into the water, I had my first beer. Slowly all the other groups came back, and we had lunch at about 12:30 p.m. Lunch was the sausage, several different salads, a potato salad, and some rolls. I was good and hungry.

Once everyone was back on board, we headed for our second dive location. I spent a lot of time on the top deck. I realized that there was a small enclosed area on the top deck that was air-conditioned and had some couches. It was also where the captain sat with the controls. It was good to get out of the sun and relax. I fell asleep for a while.

It was 3:45 p.m. when everyone got back on board. We headed back, and I got back to the hotel in time to change for NYE. I walked to the first of six bars we were going to be bused to. It got under way at 6:00 p.m. It's possible that 7:00 p.m. would have been OK too. Things started off a little slow but that didn't last long (including me). A good mixture of young people. A few more girls than boys. The drinking age in Australia is eighteen. At the second bar we went to, there was a smoking area on the second-floor outside deck. I had on my new Aussie hat that was quite a hit. A good conversation starter and did attract the ladies. I let a lot of them put the hat on. Changed the personality also.

I also lit up my cigar. This was also quite an attraction. I got some of the ladies to take a puff or two (need to see the pictures). They were calling me Crocodile Dundee. High fives and fist pumps. We stayed at each bar about one hour. I struck up some good conversations with a few of the ladies and for a good amount of time, but the younger guys won out in the end.

It was close to midnight, and there were some fireworks starting. At midnight, I was able to kiss two ladies on the lips. Not your typical friendly kiss, but a real kiss. I wasn't too far from the hotel, so at about 1:00 a.m., I walked back in not too bad a condition. When I got back to the hotel, I brought out the cabbage and made myself a Bloody Maria made with tequila and went to sleep.

Wednesday, January 1, 2014
Happy New Year

Woke up a little after 6:00 a.m. Watched some TV and went down to the lobby about 8:00 a.m. Took my breakfast, coffee, juice, and journal out to the pool and sat in the shade. It's about 10:15 a.m. now. I needed to read over my itinerary very carefully and have my less-complicated itinerary printed out. The concierge at the hotel will take care of this for me. I have nothing planned for this afternoon. The hotel concierge suggested a river-rafting trip that worked out perfectly for the afternoon. I also had the concierge confirm my shuttle pick-up for the return to the airport tomorrow morning. I am waiting to be picked up to go rafting at 2:00 p.m. now.

On the bus, we were given the usual papers to fill out and a few dos and don'ts for the rafting before we got into the rafts. We had a good and fun mixed group consisting of one Japanese man, another couple, a single young attractive woman with her fourteen-year-old boy, and me. The Japanese man and I, on either side, were in the middle, and the woman and her kid were on either side behind me. In the rafts, we were given some commands to follow and practiced them before we started. The water felt good. The guide was at the back, and we were toward the front. One of the fun things we did during the rafting was when we got close to another raft and splashed them using our paddles. The fourteen-year-old started most of them.

At several spots in the river, the rapids got very intense, and we were given instructions to get down. This command was given when there was imminent danger of falling out of the raft. There was another raft where two people did fall out of their raft but were recovered and not hurt. We all had a good laugh. Then a little farther downriver, all of us got into the river and floated ahead of the raft for a good distance. There was a photographer taking pictures of us as we went by. The kid was having the time of his life. At the end of the rafting, we got out and carried the rafts back up to the road and loaded them on a large trailer. We changed and came back out for a group picture.

On the way back on the bus, I asked the young lady if she would like to join me for a drink. She agreed. Everything was good up to this point. I knew her first name but didn't think it was necessary at the time to know her last name. She was the first one to be left off, quite a long distance from the center of town. She said she would meet me at 6:00 p.m. at my hotel. When I looked at my watch, it was 5:30. I tried to get her attention but couldn't. I was thinking about getting off the bus and should have but didn't. I did get the name of the hotel. I tried everything to get her last name, but they said they couldn't give out that info.

When I got back to the hotel, I got the front desk person to call her hotel. I gave them her first name and described who she was with and where she came from, but they insisted on having her last name. The man tried his best but no help. I went to my room and changed. I had a cold beer and mixed myself a rum and OJ. It was about 7:30 p.m. now. I brought some of the leftovers down to be heated, took them back up to my room, and watched some TV. What a blown opportunity. This would have never happened to my friend Moe. When I get back, I will ask him what he would have done and said differently. I know he will make fun of me and tell me how he would have handled it.

Thursday, January 2

Left a wake-up call for 3:30 a.m. I woke up by myself at 3:00 a.m. I didn't feel like packing the night before. I'm supposed to leave the hotel by 5:30 a.m. The hotel lost power, but I don't know for how long. I used my wristwatch for the correct time. I had time to write in my journal when the power went out again. I used a chair to prop the door open. I slowly finished packing. After I was packed, I took my bags down to the lobby and checked out. Shortly after that, the power came back on. I waited for my transportation outside. It came right on time. Got to the airport, got checked in, and went through security.

My destination was Darwin. Got to Darwin about 1:30 p.m. I have never heard of setting your watch ahead or back only thirty minutes. Took the shuttle to the hotel. I checked in. The lady told me I was staying there one night, checking out, staying one day in another place, and coming back to the same hotel the next day. A little confusing. In the meantime, I went to a shop and bought a six-pack of beer and a pint of rum. I think I've gotten most of my shopping done except for replenishing any liquids I might need. After putting things away, I brought a beer and a cigar down to the pool and wrote in my journal. It's almost 6:30 p.m. I walked down to the waterfront to have some dinner. In Darwin, I have a very full itinerary. I think it's the start of the rainy season here, but so far it hasn't rained. It does stay light longer now. I must add that I am a little sore after the rafting yesterday. After dinner, I walked back to the hotel with a to-go box. They have always come in handy later on.

Friday, January 3

Woke up the first time at 3:00 a.m. and went back to sleep. Woke up again at 6:00 a.m. I packed a few things for the day ahead. Today we went to Litchfield National Park (LNP). Picked up at the hotel at 7:10 a.m. and joined a group of twenty people. This time Moe was correct when he said that most of the people on these tours would be old. The LNP had some beautiful waterfalls and an incredible amount of termite dwellings in a part of the outback. There were two very distinct, different termite dwellings. The first one resembled the headstone of a grave. We looked at a very large field with about a foot high grass with hundreds of these headstones, and it looked like a huge cemetery. The other termite dwelling was called a cathedral structure, sometimes standing ten to twelve feet high. They were all built the same way and were all facing the same direction. All this was for a purpose. I was able to take pictures of the termites.

I didn't pay attention to my camera battery, and it went out right after that at the worst time because the next place we went to were some two-hundred-foot-high waterfalls. We were able to go into the water and wade around. I asked a guy to take some pictures of me with his camera, and I gave him my e-mail address. I hope he will send them to me. We visited another falls but not as impressive as the first one and we were not allowed to go swimming. On the way down from those falls, I saw a rock wallaby—in the kangaroo family but much smaller with large eyes—and the first of many sightings of iguanas (a very large lizard). This one was about four feet long and about six to seven feet wide at the belly.

After, we went to have lunch. At the third falls, we were not allowed to go swimming because of the possible presence of crocodiles. Because of the rainy season, when the rivers would overflow into the creeks that flowed into the falls, the crocs could get into the falls area. NO swimming. The last falls we went to were not as tall as the others, but there were several pools of water you could swim in. So I did. There was an iguana swimming in the same pool as I was literally about two feet away. I just stayed still and let her have her way. Most of the others were scattering or getting out of the pool.

There was a guy on our bus that reminded me of Billy Bob Thornton from the movie *Sling Blade*. He plays the part of a crazy killer who was released from prison and goes to a small town. The way he talked was at the end of a sentence he would give a long distinct hum or groan-type noise. This guy did the same at the end of a sentence. Kinda scary.

On the way back, there were signs that it had rained earlier from the puddles in the road and the dark clouds. We got back to the hotel about 5:30 p.m. The first thing I did was to recharge my camera battery. I am now at the pool with a beverage, writing in my journal. I went out for dinner to a fun restaurant about three or four blocks from the hotel by the name of Shenannigans. After I ate, I went back to the hotel and went to sleep. I think I will have to do some laundry soon.

Saturday, January 4

This was going to be at least a fourteen-hour day. Picked up at the hotel at 6:10 a.m. Most of it was spent traveling on the bus. The first place we stopped by was a place to get some coffee or a bite to eat if we wanted. It took us one and a half hours to get there. I had a cup of coffee. The bar was made out of wood, a beautiful long wooden bar with real iron railroad spikes stuck in the wood. Some of them were loose. So I took two of them. We then went on to a WWII memorial cemetery to honor the Australians killed in the war. The cemetery grounds were kept beautifully. I saw several large wallabies and some large geese.

After that we drove to a falls, which was very disappointing. It was about a nine-foot falls, and there were hundreds of annoying flies constantly buzzing around you. Then we were driven to have lunch with some salads and cold meats. Next we went on a river cruise that was advertised to possibly see some crocs. It was a two-hour cruise with the flies always present. It was a slow torturous boat ride. Saw a very small baby croc sunning itself on a branch near the water. The cruise was in a gorge with some high cliffs on either side. We even had to get off of one boat and walk a few yards to get on another boat to take us the rest of the way. The guide spoke very fast and with a heavier accent than normal (hard to understand). On the way back, we had to change boats again. I think any longer with the flies would have been trouble. We got back on the buses just in time and headed back to the place to have dinner where we were this morning. I will say something to the AAA agent when I get back to Houston. We finally got back to Darwin about 9:30 p.m. I'm writing in my journal now and calling it a day. This was the only bad tour of the trip, I'm glad to say.

Sunday, January 5

It is 5:30 a.m., and I'm in the lobby waiting to be picked up and taken to the next city to spend one day there and return on Monday. The plan was to pack light and bring all the rest of the things down and check out for that one day. I chose not to go through all that bother, plus having to unpack when I got back.

No thanks. I just kept the room, not check out, and yes, pay for that day. I'm glad I did.

There were a lot of activities planned for the next twenty-four hours. We left Darwin at 6:15 a.m. There were only ten of us on this tour. The day before, there were thirteen people. Today our first stop at 8:00 a.m. was at a small roadside café and restaurant to have some coffee and a bite to eat if we wanted. Then we drove to an escarpment very high up that had a lot of ancient Aboriginal drawings on the walls, some of them tens of thousands of years old. Then we drove to have lunch. The usual salads and cold meats.

Then we drove to what was called the Yellow River for another river tour in hopes of seeing some crocs. Didn't see any crocs but saw a lot of different birds, including a male and a female water eagle high up in a tree. Very much like the American eagle. This river tour was far better than the first one, without as many flies and without having to change boats, and it was a bit cooler. A lot of pictures. We were taken through a maze of smaller river passages. The tour lasted two hours.

The captain guide was much better. You could understand him. He also invited anyone who wanted to come up and have their picture taken behind the wheel. I couldn't resist. After we got off the boat, we were asked if we wanted to take a flight in a small plane (at an extra cost) and be able to see a much larger area of the land in a short time, and of course, I did. Only seven people fit in the plane. We saw some incredible falls, plateaus, and a whole lot more. The flight was as smooth as any big jet, except for a minor bit of turbulence at the end. In the distance, we could see some bad weather coming our way with some lightning. We also made some forty-five-degree angle turns. "No problem, mate."

When we landed, we were driven to the hotel to spend the night. Just after we got back to the hotel, it started to rain with no effect on the tour. There were people that did this tour in one day and driven back to Darwin. That would have been too much for one day.

Monday, January 6

When I woke up, I turned on the TV and caught one of the NFL playoff games between the Chargers and the Bengals. We got back on the bus and were driven back to Darwin. Today we left for Alice Springs for two days. We were shown some incredible Aboriginal rock art over thousands of years old, some incredible rock formations, and one mountain called Blue Mountain because at sunset the shadows on the mountain cast a deep purple color. The mountain itself was one gigantic mound-like mountain not surrounded by anything else. It stood alone. We saw a lot of this mountain, also once at sunup.

One of the highlights of the trip was a beautifully arranged dinner under the stars. We got to the location a little before sunset. We were greeted with some hors d'oeuvres and a choice of wines or champagne and a man playing one of the hollow sticks. Then we went to an area where there were tables and chairs set up for us for a dinner under the stars.

On the way out, a very attractive woman sat next to me, but she was married and her husband and two kids came along. While we had the hors d'oeuvres, I struck up a conversation with the husband. We had a lot in common. He reminded me of myself when I was his age. Enough said.

It was a very good buffet-style dinner with both white and red wine served. Plus a special surprise of a tawny port wine and cheese. During dinner, we were entertained by some Aboriginal dancers. There was also a narration about the stars and planets. After this fest, we were loaded back on the bus and back to the hotel.

The second day was very exciting. We were taken on another river cruise. This time was much, much better. On this cruise, we were able to watch some crocs actually jump up out of the water. This was done by a lady holding a long pole with some meat dangling from a short rope. The first croc was the granddaddy of them all. He was about seventy or eighty years old, about 1,500 pounds, and over fourteen feet long with a dingy yellow head and a slimy olive-green body. They got him to jump up a few times. There were about seven or eight more crocs (much smaller but in good size anyway). Again my camera batteries were down, so I asked a young couple to e-mail me some of the pictures they took. He had a very good camera. He said he would. I offered to pay him, but he refused. I hope he will send them. There were also some good-sized birds that they would lure through small pieces of meat, and they would catch them in flight. Got back to the hotel about 5:00 p.m. and did a load of wash. While that was going on, I went to the store to restock.

Tuesday, January 7

Woke up early but stayed in bed till about 10:00 a.m. Got up and caught the shuttle to the Darwin airport. I was supposed to fly from Darwin to Alice Springs. When I got to the airport, I found out that this flight was canceled because not enough people had booked that flight. The Qantas airline people were very nice and booked me into a very nice hotel and a $50 meal all at their expense and wrote a letter to the tour company explaining what had happened. So far this was the only setback. I was assured that I would not miss out on anything. I was shuttled over to the hotel and made myself at home. I didn't unpack because I was leaving early the next day. I saw an ashtray on the balcony. So I called the front desk to find out if it was permitted to smoke out there and it was. So far this was the only setback in the trip. I was booked on the first flight out on Wednesday, the eighth, at 7:10 a.m. I sat out on the balcony with a cigar and a drink. The only thing wrong with the hotels in Australia was they don't have ice machines on each floor, so I kept on having to go to the lobby bar or restaurant for ice. I sat down and wrote in my journal. Then I went to dinner and had a glass of wine with it. There were two very good tours I didn't want to miss. I looked over my schedule again very carefully. I was still OK; the only thing I missed out on was a camel ride. No big deal. I left a wake-up call for 5:00 a.m. Since I was five minutes away from the airport, this gave me plenty of time.

Wednesday, January 8

Another long day was scheduled. Got up at 5:00 a.m. and caught the shuttle to the airport. The plane left for Alice Springs at 7:10 a.m. and from Alice Springs to Ayers Rock. When I arrived in Ayers Rock, it was about 4:00 p.m., and I was driven to where the tour was. They were just starting to walk back from a scenic lookout point. I went there quickly. The guide stayed with me and explained to me what I was looking at but in a shorter version. Turned around and got on the bus with the others. From then on, I was back on schedule.

A sidenote observation: as we flew over a large part of Australia, it made me think of the first settlers that went from St. Louis to the Pacific Ocean, not knowing what to expect. The first person to successfully go from the southern tip of Australia to the northern tip in the 1860s must have encountered much of the same things. The extreme weather conditions and the savages (Indians, Aborigines) and the dangerous animals.

Back to the tour. We went on a series of gigantic rock formations. We got back on the bus and drove about one hour to watch the sunset and how it changed colors from a light orange to a deep orange color. There were some tables set up for us with some dips, spreads, chips, and raw vegetables and some wine. This was a welcome break. Some of the group went to a BBQ. I was not in that group, but the next day I was. The group I was in was shuttled to a resort where we could pick out our own steaks or sausage or shrimp to cook ourselves on a grill. This was OK. I had a beer with my meal. I talked to a couple from Ireland. They were very amusing but hard to understand. When I got back to my room, I took a shower and sat down with some tequila and my journal. It was now almost midnight, and I will be getting up in about three hours.

Thursday, January 9

Needed to get up at 3:30 a.m. to get on the bus by 4:30 a.m. to go to a place to see the sunrise. It was beautiful but not necessary. After that, we drove to several other points of interest. More Aboriginal rock art and more history about them. Went to an Aboriginal cultural center and had lunch. The usual salads and cold cuts. Were driven back to the resort at 2:00 p.m. Were dropped off at some shops close to the resort. I bought a good-sized hat pin.

There was a shuttle bus I got on that took me to where the camel rides were. There were some camels already saddled. There was a choice of a ten-minute ride or a forty-five-minute ride. I chose the ten-minute ride. Very much like a kiddy ride. All the camels were linked by a rope to each other and were led around by a man on foot. He told us about the usefulness of the camels when they were first brought to Australia back in the early 1900s and in the present day. They were one ugly animal. I should have had a turban on or a foreign legion hat on. Ten minutes was the perfect amount of time.

My next major project was to change reservations. The reason was that the Australian Open tennis matches (one of four of the grand slams of tennis) were going to take place in Melbourne at the same time I was in Sydney. Since I had been to Wimbledon many years ago, and this would make two of four, I had to go. I will go to the US Open in New York on September 8 of this year and the French Open in Paris some other time. I had to make airline reservations, hotel reservations, and get a ticket for the fourteenth. I did this all on the computer at the resort with a lot of help from the staff. It took me most of the afternoon. I was done for the day.

Friday, January 10

My next stop was to Adelaide. The first shuttle to leave the hotel was at 9:00 a.m. I talked to the guy outside to take me earlier and was glad of doing that. This was where it got a little stressful. When I checked in, there was no record of me being on this flight. After some talking and phoning, things were cleared up just in time for me to make my flight. This proves that earlier is always better and doing a lot on your own is recommended. When I got to Adelaide, I was met by a chauffeur who took me to the hotel. Very first class. Good to be back in the big city.

Got to the hotel and got settled. Went back down to the concierge desk to reconfirm the rest of my flights, but they were closed. I got directions to the nearest liquor store and bought a six-pack of beer and a pint of rum. I'm now at the pool area, writing in my journal, with a beverage.

When I woke up early this morning, I turned on the TV and caught the end of the Wild Card game between the Saints and the Eagles. The Saints won 26–24 on a last-second field goal. After I finished writing in my journal, I went out for dinner. So far the weather has been very good (hot but good).

Adelaide is on the southern coast of Australia. There are some beautiful beaches here. A lot more to do than I have time for. About one and a half million people. Went to a restaurant close by that was recommended to me on the second floor of a hotel. A very nice place. Just before going there, I went into a gaming room (casino). It had only machine-operated gambling. I put $20 into the blackjack machine and quickly won the $20 plus $50 more and quit. I had a good dinner. I talked to my waitress. Her boyfriend played guitar in a band on one of the more popular streets called Light Square with many bars with entertainment. The band was upstairs. I didn't have my Dundee hat or a cigar, so because there was plenty of time, I walked back to the hotel and got them. Before long, I was surrounded by four or five ladies. Of course they had to try the hat on and take a puff of the cigar. I didn't think to bring my camera, but there was a professional photographer there. I gave him my e-mail address and $10. I hope he will keep his word. It's 12:30 a.m., and I went back to my hotel, wrote in my journal, and went to sleep.

Friday, January 11

Picked up at the hotel at 6:15 a.m. and was driven to the ferry where we crossed over to Kangaroo Island. The crossing took two hours. Luckily, I was dressed warmly. The weather was clear but cool. I had a good hot cup of chocolate and a fruit pie. When we got off the ferry, we were transferred to a bus. Another busy day. Went to a honeybee farm. Then driven to a place to have lunch just about noon. We then drove to a place where we were able to see a lot of lions and their newborn. We were told to stay together and not to get too close.

The next stop was to a place where they had demonstrations of large predatory birds, and up close also. With a glove on, we took turns holding the birds. Then we went to a cultural center where I bought a nice jacket. It also came in handy. Our final stop was down by the water where we watched a man feed a large group of very big pelicans. They were big and ugly birds.

We then were taken to a hotel to spend the night. This was the second time we stayed one night and returned the next day. As I did before, I kept my room in Adelaide without all the bother. I also took a to-go cup with me. It came in handy.

Our hotel and dinner were already paid for. It was a little before 6:00 p.m. I noticed that the doors to one of the lounges were open and with no one around. I got my to-go cup and had it filled with ice, then went to the bar and helped myself to a double Johnny Walker scotch and walked across the street to the beach. Then I had dinner. Close to 9:30 p.m., I went to bed.

Sunday, January 12

We were picked up at 8:45 a.m. and started out for another long day. Our first stop was to an emu oil and eucalyptus oil distillery. The eucalyptus oil has multiple uses, from health to cleaning. Then we drove to the Kangaroo Island Wildlife Park. We saw some koalas (in the bear family but not bears). Got to pet them and feed them. Also some tame kangaroos. Two of them were white. They also had some peacocks walking loose. Then we drove to have lunch.

We drove through another wildlife area. Then we came to a place called Remarkable Rocks. There was a lighthouse built in 1910, but no one operated it because it was all done automatically. A lot of large and small very unusual rock formations. Took a lot of pictures at all the different stops along the way.

Then we were driven to a place called Admiral's Arch. This was also near the water. We were able to walk down a path and some steps to get to this huge nature-made archway. One could see sea lions playing in the water.

We were driven to a small town before getting back on the ferry. We had a short time to get something to eat, so I ordered a pizza to go. We got on the ferry, and I ate my pizza on the way back to the mainland. We then got on the bus back to Adelaide that took two hours. Before coming back to Adelaide, I did find a stick to take back with me. I had a lot of things to take care of. All my flights were confirmed now. I wrote in my journal at 1:00 a.m. and finished at 3:00 a.m. I will get up at 6:00 a.m.

Monday, January 13

I got up at 6:00 a.m. and took the shuttle to the airport. Arrived in plenty of time to get checked in and went to the gate. All my airline bookings are in order now. There were some mechanical problems with the plane. Luckily, they brought out another plane. We were delayed for one hour. We arrived in Sydney at 1:30 p.m. Once more, setting my watch ahead for half an hour.

After I found out the name of the hotel, I got on the shuttle. Got checked in and went to the room. I then took my itinerary back down to the concierge desk. My main objective was to charter a fishing trip on the fifteenth or sixteenth. After a few calls, we were able to book one on the sixteenth with an early morning start, 5:30 a.m. I also told them that I was not going to be able to go on the fourteenth and fifteenth day tours because I was going to Melbourne for the Australian Open. I also made reservations to have dinner on the top of their Space Needle, like the one in Seattle, Washington. My reservation was for 7:30 p.m. Had a good dinner with some wine. The view from the top was impressive as well as the view of the skyline from the plane when we came in.

Tuesday, January 14

Got up at 5:00 a.m. and caught the 6:10 a.m. shuttle that I had prearranged to go to the airport. I packed just enough for one day. A carry-on bag. Got my boarding pass. I had time for a Baileys and coffee and to write in my journal. Arrived in Melbourne at 10:30 a.m. Paid for a round-trip ticket from the airport to the main bus terminal that unknowingly was four blocks from my hotel. Got checked in. Got some questions answered at the front desk. It's about noon so I walked to the corner to a restaurant and had some lunch.

With my Australian Open tickets in hand, I caught the train a few blocks away that took me directly to the stadium and didn't have to pay a thing both ways because I had a valid ticket to the matches. Got to the stadium at 2:00 p.m. I could not get in yet because my ticket was for the 7:00 p.m. matches. I had to buy a special ticket that would get me in. After I got in, I walked around a bit and went to an Australian Open merchandise stand and bought a program that included the matches for today. A cap from the Australian Open, a lanyard for my tickets, and a hat pin of the trophy of the AO.

The matches scheduled for the evening were Rafael Nadal against someone from Australia. And the second match was Maria Sharapova against someone from the USA. I was very lucky without knowing it. I found out that there were some practice courts where there were tennis players practicing. I stuck around till they were through practicing, and on their way out, I got their autographs on the inside part of the cap I bought. I got twelve in all including the coach of Serena Williams, a French man. (I have all the names of the players listed on another sheet.) He was being interviewed at that time. I was able to talk to him in French for a short time. It was very hot, in the nineties, and humid. I had a beer or two and a lot of water. The 7:00 p.m. evening matches could only start after the last match from the afternoon was over, however long that would take, before we were allowed to go in.

Their match was over at 7:45 p.m. Shortly after that, we were allowed to go in. This was about the worst part. If you could imagine New Orleans during Mardi Gras on Bourbon Street and pack that into a hall about ten feet wide and no AC. I was able to make my way to a food court and grabbed three sandwiches to take to my seat. Then I slowly inched my way to the door I was supposed to enter and waited there for a long time until they opened that door to let us in.

The stadium was packed and the roof was open. The sun was going down now, so it began to cool down some. Still no AC to speak of. That's one thing I can't understand that a venue like that, that generates so much revenue, would not have AC and close the roof on such a day. Anyway, I made it to my seat and ate one of my sandwiches. On my left was a couple from Australia. On my right was a young lady from India. She was more modern but still had on the typical dress with the head covered but not the face. There was a group of Nadal fans dressed in Spanish colors. They would lead some Spanish cheers between points, and of course, some Aussies would counter with their own cheers. Very funny and some funny remarks every once in a while. But total silence just before the next serve.

During the first set, the Aussie asked for a medical time out. This was not a good sign. He was playing very well and his serve was faster than Nadal's. Nadal won the first set 6–4. The second set started. Partway through the set, the Aussie forfeited the match because of his leg injury. Everyone was disappointed and let him know it. A little after 10:00 p.m., the ladies took the court. The Russian won the first set, so I left and found out later that she won the second set as was expected. I caught the train back to the hotel. Got out of my clothes and took a well-needed shower. Then I ate my other sandwich and went to sleep.

Wednesday, January 15

A wake-up call for 5:00 a.m. and took the airport shuttle back to the airport. Had a screwdriver to douse my throat followed by a Baileys and coffee. This is where I am now, writing in my journal. I have nothing planned for today but will find something I'm sure. Flew back to Sydney and arrived at 10:30 a.m. Got back to my hotel and unpacked my new souvenirs. I was pretty tired, so I stayed in my room most of the day. Later on I went out to a Subway sandwich store and got a Footlong to take with me on my fishing trip. That was it for the day.

Thursday, January 16

As usual, the fishing trip started very early. To meet the guide at 5:30 a.m., I woke up at 4:30 a.m. and packed my sandwich and three beers. Took a cab to the meeting place that was very close to their landmark, Sydney Opera House, and the bridge at the harbor. The guide was an older man and had lived here all his life and has been a fishing guide for well over thirty years. His boat was not too impressive but served the purpose well.

It was still dark when we started out with a full moon behind us just above the bridge. It made for a great picture. It was a little chilly at first. After the sun came up, the chill went away. We boated around for a while to catch some squid and other bait fish. Now it was about 7:00 a.m. The water was relatively calm and not a cloud in the sky.

In the first place we stopped, we caught about four or five different kinds of fish but none we could keep. But it was good fishing. One of the fish was called a banjo shark because of its shape. The body was round like a banjo and the tail was like the tail of a shark. We moved around a few times, each time catching a few more fish. Most of them put on a good fight. The most exciting part was when we came upon a school of yellowtail kingfish. I had a good sized one on a light tackle ten-pound test line. The fish was too big and snapped the line. Another kingfish took the line of the heavier tackle. This one didn't get away. It was just two inches too short to keep. Had to throw it back. But got a good picture of it as well as the other fish. Both of the kingfish put up great fights.

During the time we were fishing, I had part of the sandwich and two beers. We fished around a few more places but with no luck. It was after 12:30 p.m. and time to go back. Overall it was a good fishing trip.

I walked back to the hotel, ate the rest of my sandwich, and drank a beer. Wrote in my journal, took a shower, watched some TV, and fell asleep. Woke up at 8:00 p.m. I got dressed and went to a nightclub, bar, and restaurant to do some more fishing—if you know what I mean. I doubt if I'll catch anything. I went to a bar that was recommended to me. I had a glass of chardonnay. I think it was too early because it wasn't very busy yet.

I looked across the street and saw a whole lot of young people going into an alleyway. So I went over to see what the attraction was. They were lined up to see some live entertainment—I think by invitation only or to have paid in advance. There were nice restaurants on both sides of the alley. I sat outside at one of them and ordered dinner. They were just about to close the kitchen. It was very good. A young German man who was in line just sat down at my table and started talking to me. We had a conversation about some very strong issues. The young man rejoined his friends. As it got later, the crowds grew larger. One could see practically every style of dresses, shapes, and sizes that passed by. I started to walk back to the hotel at 12:30 a.m. Got to the hotel and finished writing in my journal for this day.

Friday, January 17

It will be another long day because today was when I returned to Houston. I woke up several times during the night but went back to sleep. Finally woke up at 8:30 a.m. Turned on the TV to one of the NFL playoff games—New England versus Indianapolis Colts. Went down to have some breakfast. Then went back up to the room, finished packing, and watched the rest of the game. New England won 43–22.

I will go through customs in Dallas-Fort Worth (Texas). This should be a big test on what they will let me bring in. I got all my things together for the flight. The papers I needed, etc. I'm glad I glanced over the instructions for flying back international. It says to be at the airport at least three and a half hours before the flight. I had arranged for the shuttle to take me back, but I didn't think it would get me there in enough time. I went to the concierge desk to get an earlier pickup, but it couldn't be changed, and I didn't want to take a chance. So I was forced to take a cab that cost $50. A small price for peace of mind. It took about two and a half hours to get through all the checkpoints. Since I was early, everything went well. Once again, it's good to do things ahead of time and to be resourceful.

Boarded the plane. There was a slight delay in taking off. This plane was even bigger than the one I flew out on. We flew nonstop from Sydney to Dallas-Fort Worth. We took off on the seventeenth and landed on the seventeenth. I will never be able to figure out why that is possible, coming or going, even if you try to explain it to me. So don't waste your time or mine. When we landed I had a very short time to collect my bags and stick, make it through customs, and make it to catch my flight to Houston. It all worked out well. Very lucky they didn't check my bag. They did ask me about the stick. I explained to them that it was not a living thing and what I was going to do with it. I did have that kangaroo skull and two beers and the two iron railroad spikes in my bag. When I landed in Houston, I retrieved all my things, including my stick. Ron picked me up and brought me back to the Mark Condominiums. It was about 6:30 p.m. On the way back, I told Ron a little about the trip. I did get the three of them a few souvenirs from Australia. When I got back, the mail had already been picked up and put into my room. I started to unpack but sorted through my mail and checked on my e-mail. I also wrote a little in my journal but wasn't finished with it yet. Ate something, watched some TV, and fell asleep at 3:00 a.m.

Saturday, January 18

And you thought I was through with my journal. Wrong. Got up at 7:30 a.m. and in no particular order, I got on the computer and deleted a lot of my journal entries, read over some of them, had to write two checks and mail them, do some more unpacking, sort of organized some of my papers, deposited some checks (only two), and got some cash. I came back with $6 in my pocket. Took my bracelet with the shells on it to the Fast Fix to have them put the shells from Australia on the bracelet, took my camera memory chip to the CVS to have my pictures developed, and added some text on some of them. It took about two hours and the worst thing was when I was practically through, I had erased the pictures I wanted to develop but not all the pictures. So I had to start all over but not then.

I went to Michael's arts and craft shop and bought two shadow box frames—one for the skull and the other for the two railroad spikes. Oh yes, I made twelve phone calls before going out. I went across the street to Randall's to pick up some things for Sunday night when Ron, Megan, and Olivia were coming over for dinner that she was going to prepare.

There was a Walgreens in the same shopping center. So I went there and did my pictures again. When I was finished, the man said it would be tomorrow before they would be ready. There were 155 pictures that I had developed. No problem, mate. It was 8:00 p.m., and I had defrosted sausage and pork ribs. I took them down to the pool grill and grilled them with a large glass of white wine, brought them back upstairs, and had dinner. Watched some TV and fell to sleep at 3:00 a.m., got up, and went to my bed.

Sunday, January 19

I woke up at 6:30 a.m. I was dreaming that I was still traveling or flying, and when I woke up, it took me a little time to know where I am. Today I had to make two batches of Tarama and do three more steps to get them ready to take to Phoenicia's on Monday.

I went back to Walgreens to pick up my pictures. I looked forward to watching two NFL playoff games. Made some more phone calls. Had brunch with Mother. Put the two things into the shadow boxes and labeled them. Watched the first playoff game, New England versus Denver in New England. Denver won 26–16, but it was a much closer game until nearly the end.

The second game was San Francisco versus Seattle. This was the time that Ron and the gang came over for dinner. Megan prepared some pork tenders. I had bought some corn on the cob and some salad. We ate watching the game with a bottle of white wine. This was the game where Sherman of Seattle made the great defensive play to end the game and held on to win. The stunt that Sherman pulled right after the game was over. Plus the interview that he gave seconds after the game ended caused quite a controversy. I'm sure it will be talked about for the next two weeks leading up to the Super Bowl. The three left before the game was over.

Monday, January 20

Got up at 6:00 a.m. Still had the traveling dreams. Went online and paid some bills. Took about three hours, but that's me. At 11:00 a.m., brought the Tarama to the two stores. Ate lunch at 2:00 p.m. The three things I have left to do was to work on my walking stick (that will take a few days), start to type my journal, and sort out my pictures. Things are starting to get back to normal. But I will fast forward to Wednesday, January 29, and I'm all done. Will end on that note. I just hope that the people who are supposed to send me pictures will do so. I will wait for some time before I will put them in a frame. It would be a shame if they didn't. Next stop: the US Open in NYC.

Trip to San Pedro Island, Belize, and Roatán Island, Honduras, Central America
May 28 to June 8, 2014

Wednesday, May 28

The weather a few days before and that day were filled with heavy rains and flash flooding. I called that morning to check on my flight status. Everything was OK. Ron spent the night with me because we had to leave early to catch my plane. My flight left at 8:30 a.m. We got there in record time. I had time to stop at a bar and have my traditional Baileys and coffee. I did pack my suitcase well in advance, including five plastic bottles of tequila, Crown Royal, vodka, and white and red wine. My suitcase was a half-pound underweight.

The flight took about two hours. They are on East Coast time. The weather was overcast, about mideighties, and humid. A lady was waiting for me after I went through customs. She looked at my vouchers and took me to my next flight to San Pedro. At that time I also booked my return flight to Belize. My flight took off fifteen minutes later. It was a small plane for about twelve people. I sat in the back because the back two seats were like something you would find in first class.

The last person to board was a beautiful tall young lady returning to San Pedro. She works at the Phoenix hotel and resort a few yards from where I was staying. Perhaps I will try to contact her later. Again a lady met me and walked me to my hotel. It was about 11:30 a.m. now. Checked in, unpacked, put some sunscreen on, and went back out looking for some souvenirs and a hat. All the bottles made it in good shape. After shopping, I went to a small restaurant on the beach. My room has a kitchen and a small sitting room.

The lady that walked me back to the hotel met me at 3:00 p.m. at the hotel to take me to the supermarket. I bought some deli food, chips, beer, and mixers for the alcohol I had. I also bought something for her to take home to her mother. She helped me take the things back to my place and went on her way. She gave me her private phone number. I saw some people sitting on the pier just across from my room, so I made myself a drink before going out to join them. There were two couples, one of them were American, the other one was Latino. The American couple had a cute young daughter about six years old. We talked for a long time.

I also had a cigar, and I brought another one for the lady to smoke. We discussed going fishing together on Friday. At the same time we were talking, there were about four or five stingrays swimming close to the surface of the water. I took some pictures of them. At about 7:00 p.m., I went out to eat. After that, I went to a bar for a short time. Then I went back to my hotel room and went to bed.

Thursday, May 29

It's now Thursday morning, and I'm writing in my journal. I tried to sign up for cave tubing, but it was too late. So I signed up for it on Saturday, the thirty-first, and an all-day sail with snorkeling on Sunday, June 1. Whenever a fishing boat comes in and they clean the fish on the pier and throw the scraps into the water, a bunch of rays gather. The water was between ankle and knee deep. I stood in the water while the rays were feeding. The rays would glide over your feet. It felt silky, satiny, and slimy at the same time. It was fun to watch and hear the reaction of the other people, especially the women!

I did very little the rest of the day. At about 8:00 p.m., I went out to eat. After dinner, I went to a bar that was recommended to me and had a shot of tequila and talked to a very sexy lady. I might go back to that bar another time. Went back to the hotel and went to sleep.

Friday, May 30

Got up at 5:30 a.m. Put on a bathing suit, shirt, and my new hat (that gets a lot of compliments everywhere). We were due to go out fishing at 7:30 a.m. but didn't go until 9:30 a.m. (not sure why). The couple and their daughter were there. They knew the guide and his helper. The four of us split the cost of the trip. The boat was about twenty feet long, not very wide, and had a shady area to sit under. Before we left, the husband told me what beverages they were bringing. So I went back to get the bottle of Crown Royal and some beers. We all caught a good amount of fish. Some were keepers and some we threw back. About an hour into the fishing, I had a beer and they mixed their own drink. Because they knew the captain and the crewman very well, they also had a drink. After we had our first drinks, we started catching fish.

After fishing (and drinking) for three hours, we went to a place to snorkel and swim with sharks (supposedly harmless) and rays. I didn't join them because I was doing that on my sailing trip. We stayed out for another hour. The husband and wife picked up several conch shells with the conch still in them. On the way back, the captain got the conch out of their shells and put them in a bucket. When we got back to the pier, they cut up the conch and made seviche for us to eat while they cleaned the fish. It was very tasty. I brought out some white wine that we all had. They prepared the fish wrapped in foil with a lot of good seasonings. One other couple joined us. It was about 3:00 p.m. when we sat down to eat. There was plenty to eat for us all. The man that joined us gave me a real good Cuban cigar that I will pick the right time to smoke. It was after 6:00 p.m. Having had plenty to eat and drink and after a long day, I was tired. So I went to my room and lay down on the couch, watched some TV, and went to sleep. I woke up at 10:30 p.m. and went to my bed. Took some great pictures as usual. I have a lot of great pictures throughout the whole trip.

Saturday, May 31

Got up at 5:30 a.m. The plan was to go cave tubing today. The lady in charge met me at the hotel lobby to ask if I wouldn't mind sailing today and tubing tomorrow. I agreed. I will go sailing at 8:30 this morning. I had about one hour before sailing, so I am catching up with my journal. We walked to the sailboat and boarded. There were about fifteen of us. We all found places to sit on the deck. I sat toward the front of the boat (that was a mistake). We got most of the water when there was a splash. I took a picture of most of us before we sailed.

It took about ninety minutes to get to the first snorkeling spot—almost 11:00 a.m. We were given our masks and fins when we first got on board. On our first snorkeling, we saw some large turtles, rays, and assorted fish but no manatees (a huge fish). Got some great pictures. Our second snorkeling was at about 11:30 a.m.—thirty minutes later. Saw some other species of colorful fish. When we got back into the boat, we were served lunch. We could go below, and it was buffet style. A nice variety of food. I had a beer on the way to the first spot and a rum punch with lunch. We could have as many rum punches as we wanted. I took it easy until we were finished snorkeling.

In the third snorkeling, we saw some more rays and some sharks. Yes, sharks. They were not the dangerous kind, whatever that means. But it was still cool. There was one more dive after that, but I returned my gear and stayed on board and had a rum punch. There were two or three good-looking ladies, so I took some pictures of them underwater.

When we got back in, I took a shower and I went out to buy some things and had a snack. It was about eightish. I fell asleep watching TV. When I woke up, I went to my bed.

Sunday, June 1

Today I'm supposed to go cave tubing and to leave from here at 7:30 a.m. Because it was raining, they put the departure time at 9:30 a.m. I had two hours before we started. So I had a small breakfast and made myself a Bloody Maria.

We were picked up and went to a boat that took us to Belize City with one stop on the way to let off and pick up some people. This took about one and a half hours. When we landed, we went by car that took another forty-five minutes. Then we walked another twenty-five minutes with our tubes in hand. Instead of tubing for about four hours, we tubed for about two hours. There was a couple that went along with me. We had a guide that took us through the caves. After that, we headed back.

On the drive to the cave, I spotted a pile of sticks and made a mental note that it was right next to a large house painted bright yellow. When I saw the yellow house, I told the driver to stop. I got out and went to the pile of sticks and found myself my walking stick and took it back with me. It was a good one. This shows you how obsessed I am about getting a walking stick.

We got back to the dock at 5:00 p.m. The last boat leaves at 5:30 p.m. The trip back to San Pedro was a lot of fun. On the way back, there were five or six of us that sat on the top deck. The first part, there were three ladies. One of them was talking to an older couple. They talked mostly about water sports. I asked one of the girls if she had ever done any winter sports. She said yes. Then we found out that the couple were newlyweds. This prompted a number of songs that we all sang along with. Happy first anniversary and so on. Then it was someone's birthday. So we all sang "Happy Birthday to You." Then to the two girls who had boyfriends with them, we sang, "I'm SURE I'm going to get some tonight." Then it was my turn. I started to sing, "I HOPE I will get some tonight" and so on.

We landed at the first stop, and they got off and five young gay guys got on. They sat down with us on the top deck. They were not obnoxious but had a few drinks. One of them was a very happy guy. He looked Hawaiian. He was in love with my stick. I handed it to him, and he started dancing around with it but not vulgar. His name was Oz. So I named the stick Oz. They carried on about a lot of things that we all got a good laugh over. The two different parts of the boat trip back to San Pedro were very amusing and made the time go by very quickly. The other couple and I exchanged info.

Got back to my room after 7:30 p.m. Made myself some dinner from the stuff I bought and some red wine. Watched some TV and went to sleep.

Monday, June 2

Woke up at about 5:30 a.m. At about 6:30 a.m., I called the tour company because I left my small makeshift cooler on the sailboat. I could pick it up after 9:30 a.m. at their stand not far from my hotel. I had some time to kill, so I wrote in my journal catching up on about three days' worth for over one hour. I also wanted to find someone that could saw off the end of my stick to make it even. I did find a man with a saw at one of the restaurants that did it for me. I bought some tape to wrap around the plastic bags that were wrapped around my stick.

I also called the lady that walked me to the hotel when I first arrived to go to dinner with me tonight. She agreed to go at about 9:00 p.m. I heard of a restaurant but forgot the name. She came by cab and then we took the cab to that restaurant. It didn't look like a good place at all. We called the cab to come right back and take us to another place that was much better. We had a good dinner. The place was in walking distance to my hotel. We walked back, and she said good night. I slowly packed because I was leaving to go back to Belize City for one night on the third before going to Roatán, an island belonging to Honduras, the following day. Laid down on the couch, watched some TV, and fell asleep.

Tuesday, June 3

Woke up at 6:30 a.m. and flew back to Belize City for one day later that afternoon. Got checked in, and there was a nice restaurant in the hotel. Not much else to do.

Wednesday, June 4

Woke up at the usual time. My flight to Roatán was only at 4:15 p.m. I tried to get an earlier flight, but there wasn't one. The hotel where I was staying served a complimentary breakfast. So I went down and had some. I went out shopping and found a Mayan calendar coin with a thin turquoise ring around the coin and a small turtle made from a conch shell and a small shark made from a turtle shell. I will have them put on my shell necklace when I get back.

My flight took off on time. About a one-hour flight. This is where some confusion comes in about exactly where I was staying. The place I was scheduled to stay in was a hotel on the West Bay, and that is where I was taken. And that was where I was supposed to be. That place was occupied by very young kids and their young parents. There was practically nothing to do there. They didn't have me in their computer. So I stayed there for one night. I found out there was another place at the West End that was so much livelier with all the things needed for fishing and diving and night life as well.

The bungalow I was staying in was right next to the beach. Better yet, the bungalow right next to mine was shared by two sisters. One was married and one wasn't. I said hello to them, and they replied in Dutch. A short time later, we met up at the wrought iron table and chairs between our bungalows. At first it was hard to communicate, so I tried talking French. One of them spoke French. This made all the difference in the world. We started talking, but after a while, they were speaking much more fluent English.

I went out to find a fishing and diving charter. I found a guy that did both. I booked a fishing charter for Thursday, the fifth, diving for Friday, the sixth, and fishing on Saturday, the seventh. This took some time to negotiate all that was involved. The girls and I met back at the table some time later. We each brought out something to eat, and I brought the wine. Took some pictures and talked for hours (until well after dark). I think they went out after that, and I went back to my bungalow.

Thursday, June 5

I met my guy to go out fishing at 6:00 a.m. The boat was about twenty feet long and not very wide with a blue canvas top for shade. There was one other guy as a helper. We caught five tuna. They put up a good fight. Four of them were about four to five pounds. The other one was a good ten to twelve pounds.

At about 10:00 a.m., we headed to his sister's house who prepared them for us. Before going there, we stopped for me to buy some white wine. When we got there, the man cleaned the fish, and I walked around with a cup of wine. It took a little while for the lunch to be ready. We had the fish, some black beans and rice, and a salad. All very good. Then we headed back to the pier where he picked me up.

It was about 1:00 p.m. now. I went to my bungalow and went to sleep for a few hours. I was running low on supplies, so I went to the market to restock. I met up with the girls later on. There was a motorcycle rally (small but interesting) taking place on the main street. So we headed out. The bars were full and heard some good music as well. We walked up and down the strip, stopping at a few bars and had some drinks. The one that was married was a little wild and crazy. She was swinging in a rope swing that was hanging down next to the bar. They took some pictures of me in some funny moments as well. We had a lot of fun. We all headed back to our bungalows and turned in for the night.

Friday, June 6

Today was the day I went diving. We only started out at a little after 10:00 a.m. We reached our first dive location about 10:30 a.m. The man put the diving gear together for me and helped me put it on. When we were both in the water, we started our descent. With the help of the mooring line, we slowly pulled our way down. I had my usual problem of descending and being horizontal. After a while, I got better but still not as good as I would have liked to be. We saw a very large grouper swimming with us for a long time. After that, I must have gone down farther than I realized. I looked around for my guide. He was above me watching me. We had been down about forty minutes. I saw where the boat was and started slowly to surface. The water was nice and clear and not at all cold. I would say slightly cool. The man said I must have gone down over one hundred feet. It didn't feel like it. My camera was still working, but my watch (waterproof to one hundred meters or over three hundred feet) stopped working.

We were going to dive again, but I didn't feel like it. So we went back where he rented the tanks and gear, and we called it a day. It was about close to 1:00 p.m. now. He let me off at the pier where he had picked me up. My bungalow was close by. I walked back there and made myself some lunch from the stuff I bought and had an ice-cold beer. I went to sleep for about two hours. I went back out but sat in the shade near my front door and wrote in my journal.

Shortly after that, the two girls came back from their diving. They brought back a man they met on their dive. We all sat and had some wine and drinks and talked. The girls took a shower and changed. It was close to 7:00 p.m. We decided to go out to some bars and have some dinner. The guy went back to his place to change. He came back at about 7:45 p.m. We went out to look around on the main strip. There were a lot of people out at the bars and walking around. The four of us stopped at one bar that was very lively. We had a drink there and talked to some of the locals. Then we went to a small restaurant. We sat outside and had something to eat and drink. The food was very good. Then we moved on to another bar where there was a DJ playing some good music from the '80s and '90s. The four of us danced for a while. We hit two or three more bars and called it a night.

Saturday, June 7

The two sisters had to leave. It was my second day to go fishing. I met the boat at 6:00 a.m. at the usual pier. Same boat, same crew. We fished for about an hour to try and catch some small fish to use for bait. Finally, we caught a fish for bait, and shortly after that, I caught a good-sized barracuda, about six to eight pounds. We caught another bait fish, and I caught a twenty-five-pound barracuda (at least). Then we did some tuna fishing and caught a four- to five-pound tuna.

He asked me if I wanted to have his sister cook the tuna like before. I told him I would take it to another place to have it cooked. I paid him the money I owed him. He took the two barracuda and cleaned the tuna for me and put the fillets in a bag. It was only about 11:30 a.m. I went back to my bungalow and got the remaining two bottles of white wine and took them to a nearby restaurant. I talked to the chef, and he knew exactly what to do and how to cook them. I started on the first bottle of wine while I waited for the fish to be brought out.

The chef did a great job. He prepared them three different ways. Blackened, sautéed in garlic butter, and grilled with sides of mixed veggies and rice and beans. When the chef brought it out, I took a picture of him and the food. I finished almost all of it. The chef (a big black man) came out to see how everything was. I invited him to sit down and have a glass of wine with me. I told him everything was great. He had some wine, and we talked a bit. They only charged me US$10. That was quite a bargain. I left about a $30 tip.

It's now close to 3:00 p.m. I still had the Cuban cigar, so I lit it up and smoked it with the remainder of my wine. I went back to my bungalow and sat outside. Now in place of the two sisters, there were two younger girls in the bungalow next to me. I tried talking to them, but they spoke very little English. They were going out later to meet some friends and going home the next day. It was time to call it a day. I was leaving the next day.

Sunday, June 9

I woke up early and packed. I needed the two very nice beach bags with zippers at the top I bought one day from a lady selling them on the beach. I was able to fill them with clothes. I could put one in the overhead and one under my seat and not have to pay any extra. At about 8:30 a.m., I took a walk around. There was hardly anyone on the streets. As I passed a restaurant, I saw a nice small black sign with white lettering—"No guts, no glory"—with a skull and two cutlery crossing, also in white and Roatán, printed on the bottom. I was able to pry it loose.

A little farther down the road was the restaurant. I had lunch prepared for me. It was open with only a clean-up lady there. At the end of the bar was a fish carved out of wood about one inch thick and about one foot long and was not attached to anything. So I got two very nice souvenirs. Brought them back and packed them. I checked out of the bungalow and was driven to the airport in a complimentary shuttle.

I got to the airport in plenty of time and got checked in. My large suitcase was a half pound underweight. The flight back to Houston took about two hours. The only time there was any turbulence was taking off for Houston and landing in Houston. Megan picked me up at the airport. I made it through customs without having to open anything. The lady asked me what the long thing was. I told her it was a walking stick. I did have some alcohol in my suitcase. Over all, it was a very fun and successful trip. But I'm not sure if I would go back.